14 SECRETS

TO

BETTER

PARENTING

14 SECRETS TO BETTER PARENTING

Powerful Principles from the Bible

Dave Earley

BARBOUR
PUBLISHING

The author is represented by literary agent Les Stobbe.

Published by Barbour Publishing, Inc., P.O. Box 719, Uhrichsville, Ohio 44683
www.barbourbooks.com

Our mission is to publish and distribute inspirational products offering exceptional value and biblical encouragement to the masses.

Member of the
Evangelical Christian
Publishers Association

Printed in the United States of America.

Dedication

To Cathy, the world's best parenting partner.
It has been quite an adventure,
and I would not have wanted to take it with anyone else.

To Daniel, Andrew, and Luke,
three amazing young men.
I am very proud of you guys and am confident
that He who began such a good work in you
"will bring it to completion at the day of Jesus Christ"
(PHILIPPIANS 1:6).

Contents

1 Establish the Right Target

As I walked out of the hospital into the cool, late night air, my head was spinning. Moments earlier I had witnessed the miracle of birth and had experienced the amazing privilege of holding Daniel, our firstborn son. He was tiny, weighing six pounds two ounces. As I crossed the parking lot, I could not get the image of his little face out of my mind.

Myriad emotions swept over me. I was afraid, excited, ecstatic, humbled, and exhausted all at once. A numbing sense of responsibility pumped adrenaline into every step. I was keyed up and wide awake all the way home and through what remained of the night.

Parenthood!

That little baby boy was depending on Cathy and me for everything.

I was now officially a parent. The words *Dad*, *Dada*, *Poppa*, and *Father* swam across my mind, as did some persistent questions.

What do I do now?

Can I really handle this?

Will Cathy and I do this right?

What if we mess up?

I began to search for answers. For the next couple of years, as two more little boys were born into our family, I read books, asked questions, and watched video seminars about parenting. Yet it seemed as if something was lacking.

Then I remembered the source from which I had discovered the answer to all truly important questions—the one book that alone explained the meaning of life and gave the best answers to questions about human nature, relationships, marriage, money, work, world events, and even the future. So I began to search the Bible to learn what God said about parenting.

Trusting the Ultimate Expert

Why shouldn't we view God as the ultimate expert on parenting? After all, He is our heavenly *Father*. And after all, it was He who created children, parents, and families in the first place. As the only eternal and everywhere present (omnipresent) being, hasn't He observed every family in history? As the all-wise, all-knowing God, isn't He alone the only One who fully understands every type of child, home, and parent? With such an expert available, why search anywhere else?

On top of that, God has not chosen to keep His expertise to Himself. Instead, He generously shares His knowledge with us in the Bible. This amazing, ancient book speaks with astounding timelessness and astonishing accuracy on dozens of subjects, including parenting.

Finding the Treasure Chest—and More

One summer at the church where I am the lead pastor, I decided to teach through the book of Proverbs on Sunday mornings. In order to lay a foundation for teaching, I began reading the Proverbs repeatedly. As I immersed myself in this divinely inspired book of practical wisdom and insight, I got chills, as if I had stumbled onto a buried treasure—but even better.

Woven throughout the dozens of pages of life lessons, I discovered ancient, fundamental, nonnegotiable parenting principles. These "secrets" have served as a common denominator of successful parenting for nearly three thousand years.[1] When followed, these inspired insights produce wise children and happy parents (Proverbs 10:1). After mining the riches of Proverbs, I continued my search throughout the rest of the Bible until I had identified fourteen timeless secrets for better parenting.

The Test of Experience

I believe these secrets are trustworthy because they come from the Word of God. Furthermore, I believe in these principles because I have seen how reliably they have worked in the lives of dozens of families I have observed in my years as a pastor. Beyond that, I have confidence in them because of what I have seen in my own children.

It was more than twenty years ago that I first made a list of biblical parenting principles. You should know, however, that Cathy and I did not always follow these principles as well as we would have liked. Too often we learned the value of these secrets the hard way. Beyond that, each of our three sons has faced some rather unique and challenging circumstances. As a result, we endured some incredibly difficult times. But overall we did the best we could to practice these biblical principles.

Today we can humbly and joyously say that all three of our sons are living lives that honor the Lord. They will soon all be college graduates. All three sense a calling to vocational ministry, and at least two plan to become pastors. God has honored our efforts by giving us three amazing young adult sons. Praise His name!

God's Target for Parenting

The legend of Robin Hood conjures images of lush forests, brave men, evil villains, a beautiful woman, a generous hero, and long draw bows. Imagine a marksman so skilled that he could hit the dead center of the bull's-eye and then split the first arrow with his next shot!

Of course, anyone could outshoot the great Robin Hood under the right circumstances. Simply blindfold him and spin him around a few times. Obviously, no one can hit a target they can't see.

Better parenting begins by focusing on the right target. Do you know God's target for your parenting efforts?

You don't have to search the Proverbs long or hard before you will run into God's goal for children. In the first four verses of chapter 1, Solomon uses a variety of synonyms to make a single point: The goal is *wisdom*.

> *These are the wise sayings of Solomon. . .written down so we'll know how to live well and right, to understand what life means and where it's going; a manual for living, for learning what's right and just and fair; to teach the inexperienced the ropes thanksand give our young people a grasp on reality.*
> PROVERBS 1:1–4 MSG

The purpose of the book of Proverbs is to give direction to the young. In ancient Israel, children received most of their education at home. In adolescence, girls primarily learned domestic duties from their mothers, while the boys were placed under the tutelage of their fathers to learn character and the principles of effective living inherent in the Proverbs. One word summed up the goal of all instruction: *wisdom*.

Get Wisdom!

Proverbs is unique in that it is written from the perspective of a parent giving words of encouragement and instruction to a child.[2] For example, chapter 4 of the ultimate parenting manual opens with these words:

> *Hear, O sons, a father's instruction, and be attentive,*
> *that you may gain insight, for I give you good precepts;*
> *do not forsake my teaching.*
> PROVERBS 4:1–2

Unlike most of the modern English translations, Eugene Peterson really captures the urgency reflected in the original Hebrew when the father cries:

> *Sell everything and buy Wisdom! Forage for Understanding!*
> *Don't forget one word! Don't deviate an inch! Never walk*
> *away from Wisdom—she guards your life; love her—*
> *she keeps her eye on you. Above all and before all, do this: Get Wisdom!*
> PROVERBS 4:5–7 MSG

Wisdom is the goal of life. It is the foundation on other decisions and behavior are to be grounded. Wisdom the pathway toward skillful and successful living. It frames a way of living that pleases God. Wise parents focus their parenting on developing wise children.

Secret #1
Establish the right target: wisdom.

Skillful Living

The word *wisdom* is found more than 120 times in the book of Proverbs. But what does it mean? In its purest sense, the word most often translated "wisdom" means *skill*, *ability*, *expertise*, *competence*, *aptitude*, or *proficiency*. For example, the same word is used in Exodus to describe the technical ability involved in making the garments to be used by the high priest (28:1–3) and the expertise used in crafting the sacred articles used in the tabernacle (31:2–5).

Proverbs uses *wisdom* in a much broader and down-to-earth sense to speak of *skill in daily living*. It recognizes that people make decisions, choose friends, determine behaviors, handle their money, work jobs, raise families, and go about life with varying degrees of proficiency. Proverbs provides the advice needed to handle all of these aspects of life more effectively. So wisdom includes *common sense*.

Beyond that, Proverbs adds a moral and spiritual sense to wisdom. True wisdom is God-centered. It involves godly integrity. In some cases, it is used interchangeably with *righteousness*. So wisdom also consists of *character*.

In sum, wisdom speaks of the ability to handle life with common sense and character. But there is more. Proverbs states that real wisdom *comes from God*.

> *The fear of the LORD is the beginning of knowledge;*
> *fools despise wisdom and instruction.*
>
> PROVERBS 1:7

True skill in living begins with God and ends with God. The wise start by going to God and making Him central in their lives. They learn to see and respond to all of life from God's point of view. Wisdom is God's way of living.

Happiness and Health

In an informal survey of roughly one hundred parents, I asked, "What do you want most for your children?" Overwhelmingly, the most common response was this: "We just want them to be happy and healthy." If that is your goal, then let me assure you, wisdom is the path.

> *Happy (blessed, fortunate, enviable) is the man who finds skillful and godly Wisdom, and the man who gets understanding [drawing it forth from God's Word and life's experiences]. . . . {Wisdom} is a tree of life to those who lay hold on her; and happy (blessed, fortunate, to be envied) is everyone who holds her fast.*
>
> PROVERBS 3:13, 18 AMP

True happiness is always and ultimately the result of a right relationship with God and His world. It is an *outcome* of skillful (wise) living. It is seeing and responding to all of life from God's point of view.

Let me give you a word of caution though. Remember that *wisdom* is the goal; *happiness* is merely a by-product. Do not reverse that equation. Parents who make their children's immediate happiness the goal of their parenting are making a huge mistake. If happiness becomes the primary target, character flaws will go uncorrected and behavioral problems will be overlooked. The children will be spoiled and overindulged. The children will grow up lacking the ability to control their desires and failing to accept and skillfully fulfill their responsibilities. The parents will inevitably neglect discipline, put off needed confrontation, and fail to gain the respect they need for truly parenting their children.

If you want to raise children who will become blessed and happy adults, focus your parenting on developing their wisdom. Help them start with God, continue with God, and end with God. Teach them to live skillfully with good common sense and godly character. Help them learn to see and respond to all of life from God's point of view.

Giving your children the gift of wisdom is a great gift indeed. Wisdom bears not only the fruit of happiness but also the fruit of vitality, sound health, financial stability, and honor.

Blessed is the one who finds wisdom. . .for the gain from her is better than gain from silver and her profit better than gold. She is more precious than jewels, and nothing you desire can compare with her. Long life is in her right hand; in her left hand are riches and honor. Her ways are ways of pleasantness, and all her paths are peace. She is a tree of life to those who lay hold of her; those who hold her fast are called blessed.
PROVERBS 3:13–18

Who wouldn't want their children to enjoy good living, health, financial blessings, and honorable recognition? They are all by-products of wisdom. Wise parents focus their parenting on developing wisdom in the lives of their children.

Miss All the Bad Stuff

No parents hold their precious little baby in their arms and dream that the child will one day die homeless under a bridge. They don't hope their child will have a series of ugly divorces or leave a trail of illegitimate offspring. They can't picture their sweet little girl becoming a prostitute or sticking needles in her arm as a drug addict. They never imagine their son growing up to rape an innocent young woman. They can't conceive of their little bundle of joy behind bars as a criminal. No Christian parents want their son to grow up to become a philosophy professor who delights in turning his students away from God.

Yet it happens.

One of wisdom's many benefits is that if a child gets on the pathway of wisdom and does not veer off, he or she will avoid many damaging and deadly detours.

Hear, my son, and accept my words, that the years of your life may be many. . . . When you walk, your step will not be hampered, and if you run, you will not stumble. Keep hold of instruction; do not let go;

guard her, for she is your life. Do not enter the path of the wicked,
and do not walk in the way of the evil.

PROVERBS 4:10–14

Elsewhere in Proverbs, we find that wisdom will protect children from living a life of crime (1:8–33), wickedness (2:12–25; 4:18), immorality (2:16–18; 5:1–14; 6:20–23; 7:1–27), laziness (Proverbs 6:6–11), and poor decisions (9:13–18).

Jesus Increased in Wisdom

The Bible has very little to say about Jesus' growing-up years. In fact, most of His childhood is summarized in two sentences:

And the child grew and became strong, filled with wisdom.
And the favor of God was upon him. . . . And Jesus increased
in wisdom *and in stature and in favor with God and man.*

LUKE 2:40, 52 (EMPHASIS ADDED)

Notice that the focus of Jesus' childhood was. . .wisdom!

I encourage you to make wisdom your parenting target. As you finish reading this chapter, put down the book for a few moments and pray. If possible, have your mate join you. Unite your hands and your hearts. Ask God to help you cooperate with His plan for developing wisdom in the lives of your children. Ask Him to help you be a wise person and to raise wise children. This is a prayer that God wants to answer.

> *If any of you lacks wisdom, you should ask God, who gives generously to all without finding fault, and it will be given to you.*
> JAMES 1:5 NIV

Notes

1. I refer to the Bible principles of parenting as "secrets" because, in today's world, these principles are tragically overlooked and underapplied.

2. The phrase "My son" or "My sons" is used twenty-seven times in Proverbs (1:8, 10, 15; 2:1; 3:1, 11; 4:1, 10, 20; 5:1, 7, 20; 6:1, 20; 7:1, 24; 8:32; 19:27; 23:15, 19, 26; 24:13, 21; 27:11; 31:2).

Focus on Training

If you are the parent of young children, brace yourself for the inevitable—cuddly babies turn into challenging teenagers. As a parent who has raised three kids through the teenage years, I have observed a variety of priorities among parents.

Some work to promote their child as a future supermodel or professional athlete. Others push their children to get straight A's. Some seem to make it a priority to please their children. Others focus on providing all of their kids' needs *and* wants. Many see their job as protecting their children from any and every harmful or negative influence.

What does the Bible say our priorities should be as parents? Where should our focus be? What does God expect us to do?

The corrective lens of Proverbs brings parenting back into focus.

> *Train up a child in the way he should go;*
> *even when he is old he will not depart from it.*
> PROVERBS 22:6

Our focus as parents must be on pointing our kids in the right direction. We must deliberately and diligently prepare our children to live lives of wisdom.

Secret #2
Focus on training your children to walk in wisdom.

What Does It Mean to Train Up a Child?

Training children to walk in wisdom involves guiding, teaching, showing, encouraging, coaching, correcting, and supporting them as they learn to make their way in the world. The remaining chapters of this book will focus on twelve essential elements of good training: laying a proper foundation (chapter 3), setting a good example (chapter 4), understanding the main obstacle (chapter 5) and correcting it (chapter 6), communicating (chapter 7), praying (chapter 8), getting your children involved in ministry (chapter 9), teaching them God's Word (chapter 10), encouraging them (chapter 11), dedicating them back to God (chapter 12), and leading them to experience God for themselves (chapter 13). And when all else fails, more prayer (chapter 14).

Training is an active, intentional, involved, varied, cooperative, directed, flexible, ongoing, and rewarding process. Let's examine this process in more detail.

Nine Elements of Effective Training

1. Effective training is active.

Raising children to walk in wisdom does not just happen. It is the result of active training. When Proverbs 22:6 says, "*Train up* a child," it uses an imperative verb, which commands action. Parents must have initiative and take action.

The world, the flesh, and the devil continually seek to ensnare our children and keep them from the way of wisdom. On their own, children will not develop into wise adults. They need parental guidance, which is why God placed them in families. Left to their own devices, the predictable outcome is shame (see Proverbs 29:15).

Parents cannot passively observe their children's development. Wisdom is an acquired skill, and parents must work hard to help their children develop it. Having a great aim is important, but so is pulling the trigger. God's aim for our parenting is producing wise children, but this will not occur until we focus on training and take action.

Start now. Do not wait. Turn your good intentions into effective actions.

2. Effective training is intentional.

I have often heard parents say that they just do their best and hope everything turns out all right in the end. If their children don't become drug addicts or criminals, these parents will feel as if they have done a pretty good job.

You won't find such a haphazard, whistling-in-the-dark approach to parenting in the Bible. Training a child *in the way he should go* suggests a specific direction, a purposeful plan for pointing the child toward wisdom.

Just as no wise person would try to build a house without good blueprints, no wise parent should try to raise a child without following God's plan. The "way" in Proverbs 22:6 refers to God's way, the way of wisdom.

3. Effective training requires involvement.

Many Christian parents center their training on one primary act: taking their children to church. Though this is certainly part of a biblical approach to training children, by itself it is not enough. In today's world, a child whose training involves little more than a couple hours of church each week is probably not going to develop the skills of wise living. We all know people who "grew up in church" but are failing to walk in wisdom as adults.

Training requires personal, one-on-one involvement, and it takes time. It is a daily investment in the life of your child.

4. Effective training is varied.

In the Old Testament, the Hebrew word for *train* has several shades of meaning. It comes from a root word meaning "the roof of the mouth"—the same word used to describe the practice of placing a rope bridle in a horse's mouth in order to break the horse. It means to curb, to break, to bring under control. In a sense, it captures perfectly the idea of bringing the wild spirit of a child under control.

The word *train* is also used to describe the practice of a midwife rubbing sour grape juice on a newborn's gums, lips, and roof of the mouth in order to "train" the baby to nurse. This speaks to the motivational elements of training. Parents must *stimulate* a child's thirst for wisdom, righteousness, and learning.

Cathy and I used a variety of methods to positively motivate our children toward wisdom. We gave monetary rewards for activities such as chores, memorizing scripture, and reading good books. We blended field trips and mission trips with family vacations. We set an example by showing interest in art, music, literature, and Christian service.

I once heard a wise pastor say that leaders are readers. To stimulate his teenage son to become a reader, the pastor paid him ten dollars for every book he read from an established list. He quipped that parents who pay their sons to take out the trash are training them to be garbagemen, "but I am training mine to be a leader."

Effective training involves a balance between positive stimulation and proper correction.

5. Effective training is a cooperative effort.

Though they may not admit it, many Christian parents attempt to parent alone, without really seeking God's help. That is clearly not parenting with wisdom. Why go it alone? It should be a great relief to know that our children are first of all God's children, and that He is more concerned about their developing wisdom than we are. Our job as parents is to cooperate with God in the process.

The word *train* also means "to dedicate." It is used to describe the dedication of a house (Deuteronomy 20:5) and the temple in Jerusalem (1 Kings 8:63).

Many Christian parents publicly dedicate their children to the Lord in a ceremony at their church. This is a wonderful and precious time for all involved. But this act of dedication must be an *ongoing reality* and not merely a one-time ceremony. As parents, we need to dedicate our children to God *daily* and pray for them. We also need to dedicate *ourselves* daily to God in order to be wise parents.

Every morning when I pray, I give my kids back to God. I ask Him to give Cathy and me the wisdom we need to cooperate with

Him in training our boys to walk in the way of wisdom. When the boys were younger, I prayed with them at bedtime, and together we asked God to help them grow up to be men of wisdom.

6. Effective training is directed.

A common mind-set in our society is that we prepare our kids to operate in the world by exposing them to the world. Proverbs, however, cautions us to carefully direct a child's exposure to the world.

The word *train*, as used in the Old Testament, has a further sense of "narrowing" or "choking." No, this does *not* mean that we can choke our kids when they act up. It *does* mean that the training process involves narrowing or restricting a child's options.

With the explosion of media and technology options, kids today are exposed to far too much sin and temptation far too early in life. These temptations present themselves in a multitude of deceptively attractive opportunities. Effective training includes limiting the temptations our children face.

In a military boot camp, learning to obey is considered essential for accomplishing the unit's mission—and, ultimately, preserving lives. Not that we are to run our homes like boot camps; but in the midst of a permissive society, we must include directive discipline in our training.

God warns against exposing our children to unnecessary evil. In the words of the apostle Paul, "Be wise as to what is good and innocent as to what is evil" (Romans 16:19). All sin is costly and leaves scars. Innocence lost cannot be regained. Sins sown in adolescence yield an ugly harvest in adulthood. Limiting exposure to evil is wise parenting.

Too many parents are reluctant to say no to their kids. Let's not forget that *we* are the parents. God has entrusted us with the serious responsibility of training our kids—and that includes setting limits and saying no.

Wise parents use boundaries, foresight, words, and discipline to direct their children in the way of wisdom and *away* from folly.

Children with clear boundaries are securer than kids without them. My boys would visibly relax when they had tested a boundary and found it firm. A warm, loving, positive *no* can be a hedge of protection around a young life.

7. Effective training is ongoing.

When Proverbs says to train a *child*, how old is a child? When does our training time end?

In the Bible the word *child* refers to someone from infancy all the way up to adulthood. In Genesis Joseph is described as a child when he is seventeen years old (37:2), and Shechem is referred to as a child when he is old enough to marry (34:19).

Children need regular, active, and balanced parental training in the way of wisdom from infancy to adulthood. The training process is ongoing for as long as the child is under the parents' roof—and in some sense it will continue throughout life.

My eldest son recently became engaged to be married. Just prior to his engagement, we had some of our most fruitful training opportunities as we talked about marriage and the importance of treating his wife with love and respect. When he was younger, he wasn't interested in such a conversation. But now he hung on every word.

8. Effective training is individualized.

Proverbs 22:6 also teaches that our parenting plans must be *individualized* to match each child. One size does not fit all. The phrase "in the way he should go" means "in keeping with" or "according to" the child's personality and his or her stage of life or degree of development.

Children are like snowflakes. Even though they have much in common, we must recognize that each child is still totally unique. Our training efforts must consider differences of personalities, learning styles, talents, gifts, interests, abilities, drives, and desires.

I have three sons. All are the product of the same two parents.

They grew up in the same country, state, town, and house. They are close in age and have experienced essentially the same events. Growing up, they ate the same food and attended the same church. Because of hand-me-downs, they have, in some cases, worn the same clothes. Yet in many ways they are as different as can be.

Our eldest is a stubborn, opinionated, driven, passionate leader, who is always ready to play. Our youngest is a thinker. More of an introvert, he loves to read and analyze. Our middle son is very sensitive, always quick to sense and respond to the hurts and needs of others. He can make friends with anyone and can talk his way out of anything. For as much as they have in common, our boys are in many ways very different.

Because every child is an individual, our training of our children must be creative and flexible, considering the unique "bent" that God has given each one. We need to train "in the way of" or "according to" the child's individual characteristics and stage of development. Knowing our kids is essential for training them effectively.

9. Effective training is rewarded.

The last part of Proverbs 22:6—"even when he is old he will not depart from it"—is one of the most quoted and most misunderstood phrases in the Bible. Often I hear Christian parents refer to it as a promise that their wayward children will one day return to God. "After all," they say, "we took them to church when they were little."

When their children show no sign of turning back to God, the parents get discouraged. Has God failed to keep His promise? No, they have simply failed to accurately interpret this verse.

First, the maxims of Proverbs are not so much promises as they are *observations* or *descriptions* of common results of certain actions. In Proverbs 22:6 the observation is that active, intentional, involved, varied, cooperative, directed, individualized training will usually result in a child who remains on the way of wisdom.

Second, the phrase "when he is old" is often misunderstood. Does it describe a middle-ager, a senior citizen, or a centurion? The correct answer is none of the above. The word for *old* means "hairs on the chin" or "old enough to shave." So, this verse refers to an adolescent. In other words, "Train up a child in the way he should go, and when he is *old enough to start making his own decisions*, he will not turn from it."

Teenage rebellion is *not* inevitable. A child placed on the road to wisdom should remain on it through the teen years. Even when teens begin to veer off track, they usually don't go so far that they can't quickly adjust back to the center of the path of wisdom.

Furthermore, the verse says that the well-directed child "will not turn from it." It doesn't say that a wayward child will one day "*re*turn" to it. The child discussed in Proverbs 22:6 never gets far from the way of wisdom in the first place. Children who have been properly trained in the way of wisdom will *stay on it* through adolescence and into adulthood. They don't have to *return* to the Lord because they never left Him.

Certainly, there are children who, despite a good upbringing, rebel as teens and later return to God. But Proverbs 22:6 is not describing those situations. It describes the outcome of continual training in the way of wisdom—training that is an active, intentional, involved, varied, cooperative, sustained effort. Such training is rewarded as the parents see their children continuing in the way of wisdom.

A Look in the Mirror

Evaluate your focus on training by answering the following questions:

1. Do I consistently focus my parenting on training in wisdom?
2. How actively involved am I with my children? How much did we talk today?
3. Have I prayed for my kids today? Do I consistently dedicate

them to the Lord and pray for their progress in the way of wisdom?

4. Do I tend to have a one-size-fits-all approach to training?

5. Am I balanced in the amount of negative limitation and positive stimulation I use in my parenting? What positive stimulation have I used in the past week?

6. If I am not pleased with my response to these questions, what specifically do I plan to do about it today?

3   Lay a Proper Foundation

When my son Daniel was four or five years old, he came home from Sunday School one week singing at the top of his lungs. As both his brothers soon joined in the singing and began to march around the living room, I noticed the deep, practical significance of their song.

The wise man built his house upon the rock,
The wise man built his house upon the rock,
The wise man built his house upon the rock,
And the rains came tumblin' down.

The rains came down and the floods came up,
The rains came down and the floods came up,
The rains came down and the floods came up,
And the house on the rock stood firm.

The foolish man built his house upon the sand,
The foolish man built his house upon the sand,
The foolish man built his house upon the sand,
And the rains came tumblin' down.

The rains came down and the floods came up,
The rains came down and the floods came up,
The rains came down and the floods came up,
And the house on the sand went SPLAT!

Facts about Foundations

When we started a new church years ago, we met in a school for the first few years. When we outgrew the school, we bought land and built a building in which to worship. To save money, we built it ourselves, and I served as the general contractor. In the process, I learned a great deal about the importance of foundations.

1. Good foundations are essential for the health and well-being of buildings. They are also essential for the health and well-being of people.

2. Buildings cannot stand much stress or pressure without a solid foundation. People also cannot withstand the storms of life without a solid foundation.

3. Just as a building's strength depends proportionately on the strength of its foundation, so does the strength of a person depend on the quality of his or her foundation.

4. The greater the height of the building, the more important

its foundation. Likewise, if you want your children to climb high in life, you must establish a solid foundation on God's Word.

5. A building's foundation is not readily visible, yet it is essential. Likewise, the foundation you establish in your children's lives may not be immediately noticeable when they are very young, but it is essential for the strength, growth, and quality of the rest of their lives.

Wise parents understand the importance of laying a foundation, the *right* foundation, in the lives of their children. But what is the right foundation?

The Right Foundation

On three separate occasions, the book of Proverbs tells us that the fear of the Lord is the beginning of wisdom (Proverbs 1:7; 9:10; 15:33). That is, respect, reverence, and obedience are the foundation of a successful life. Any discussion of parenting that neglects this essential foundation will ultimately undermine the process. Proverbs views the fear of the Lord as the root system needed for raising children who will become mighty oaks for the Lord. It is the foundation for building the necessary character for children to become wise adults.

What Is the Fear of the Lord?

When Proverbs discusses the fear of the Lord, it refers to three major facets that we might call the three Rs—respectful apprehension, reverential submission, and righteous living.

1. Respectful apprehension

"What is the single most important quality needed to become a good electrician?" I asked my friend Jim who trains electricians.

Without hesitation, he replied, "A healthy fear of electricity. Electricity is not a toy to be played with. It is an awesome power that we must fully cooperate with. Otherwise, we can put ourselves and many others in great danger."

So it is with God. He is an awesome, powerful person, whom we must respect and cooperate with. He holds the keys of life and death. He is not someone with whom to trifle; rather, He is someone to fear (Hebrews 10:31; 12:28–29). We must teach our children to take God very seriously.

2. Reverential submission

God—not man—is the center of the universe. He is the King of kings and the Lord of lords. Fear of the Lord involves making God the center of our lives. He is to be our top priority. He is the only being in the universe who deserves our complete obedience. As Proverbs 15:33 says, "The fear of the LORD is instruction in wisdom, and *humility* comes before honor" (emphasis added). Jesus modeled this humility when he prayed in Gethsemane, "Not as I will, but as you will" (Matthew 26:39). We must teach our children not to take themselves too seriously, but to take God *very* seriously.

3. Righteous living

Throughout the Old Testament, the concepts of *fearing God* and *righteous living* often are used synonymously (Leviticus 19:13–14; 25:17; Deuteronomy 17:19; Psalm 34:14). In Proverbs the fear of the Lord and departing from evil are linked repeatedly.

> *Do not be wise in your own eyes;*
> *fear the Lord and depart from evil.*
> PROVERBS 3:7 NKJV

> *The fear of the Lord is to hate evil.*
> PROVERBS 8:13 NKJV

> *By the fear of the Lord one departs from evil.*
> PROVERBS 16:6 NKJV

It is possible to sum up the concept of fearing God as making God central and taking Him seriously. Our success as parents depends in part on whether our children learn to take God seriously. If they do, wisdom will flow from this strong foundation. If they don't, folly and sorrow are the natural result. So how do we help our kids take God seriously?

Teaching Your Children to Fear God

Fortunately, Proverbs gives us some insight into how to develop the fear of the Lord in our children.

1. Teach them to take God's Word seriously.

> *My son, if you accept my words and store up my commands within you, turning your ear to wisdom and applying your heart to understanding. . .and if you look for it as for silver and search for it as for hidden treasure, then you will understand the fear of the Lord and find the knowledge of God.*
>
> PROVERBS 2:1–5 NIV

Notice the conditional nature of this passage—*if. . .then*. Proverbs 2 tells us we must take God's Word seriously if we want to develop the fear of the Lord. That means being receptive to it, memorizing it, giving it our full attention, aggressively applying it to our lives, praying over it, and studying it.

As parents, we must act as models and mentors for our children, monitor their growth in God's Word, and motivate them and show them how to read, study, memorize, meditate on, and apply scripture. We must encourage their interest in, study of, and obedience to the Bible. In God's eyes, how we treat His Word reflects how we treat Him. Fear of the Lord begins with taking God's Word seriously.

2. Lead them to know God personally.

> *The fear of the Lord is the beginning of wisdom,*
> *and knowledge of the Holy One is understanding.*
> PROVERBS 9:10 NIV

The greatest privilege in life is leading a child into a personal relationship with God. As a Christian leader, I have had the privilege of leading dozens of people into a personal relationship with Christ. Yet my most precious evangelistic experiences have been praying with my own sons when they asked Jesus to be their personal Lord and Savior.

That is merely the beginning, however. We must also help our children continue to grow in their relationship with God.

Knowing God yields four primary benefits:

1. eternal life (John 17:3);
2. wisdom and true understanding (Proverbs 9:10);
3. confidence in God's character (Jeremiah 9:23–24); and
4. spiritual strength and stability (Daniel 11:32).

Knowing God is the result of meeting several requirements:

1. an active desire to know Him (Jeremiah 29:12–13);
2. stillness in His presence (Psalm 46:10);
3. faith and diligence (Hebrews 11:6);
4. confession and cleansing from sin (James 4:7–8); and
5. experiencing Him and taking refuge in Him (Psalm 34:8).

Here are some practical suggestions for leading your children into a personal knowledge of God:

1. Pray with them daily.
2. Discuss and apply the sermon on the way home from church each week.
3. Talk about God in the course of life.

4. Refer to God as a person with feelings and desires.

5. Always speak of God as someone you love deeply and respect sincerely.

6. Share what you are learning as you grow in your own relationship with God.

7. Model a firm faith in God, and actively trust Him in hard times.

3. Show them how to walk uprightly.

To fear the Lord is to hate evil; I hate pride and arrogance,
evil behavior and perverse speech.
Proverbs 8:13 niv

Whoever fears the Lord walks uprightly,
but those who despise him are devious in their ways.
Proverbs 14:2 niv

By the fear of the Lord one turns away from evil.
Proverbs 16:6

Parents often communicate to their children the idea that avoiding punishment is the highest motive for not doing wrong.

But that is wrongheaded thinking. Evangelist Harold Vaughan says, "The fear of the Lord means to love what He loves and to hate what He hates. . . . It is a dreading of sin itself and not just its punishment."

A pastor once shared with me that as he was driving by an adult bookstore with some of the leaders of his church, one man remarked that he would like to go into one of those places sometime if he knew he wouldn't get caught. Such an attitude is far from the fear of the Lord and the way of wisdom. We fear the Lord when we truly love what He loves (righteousness) and hate what He hates (sin), *whether we get caught or not.*

When we allow unrighteousness to serve as entertainment, we weaken our children's fear of the Lord. When our kids see us laugh at sin, they learn not to take God all that seriously. This erodes the foundation of wisdom. I'm all for quality entertainment, and I believe God is the author of joy, but we must be careful not to allow our permissive culture to condition us to view sin as a form of entertainment.

I believe God will allow situations in which your kids can see that doing right is not always easy or painless. When you nevertheless model right behavior, you help lay the foundation for upright living. Your children desperately need to see that.

There will be times when honesty and righteousness will be

difficult for your kids. If you have taught them the difference between right and wrong, you must not let them off too easily just because they are children.

For example, one of my boys stole something from a friend and lied about it. He was only three and a half at the time, but he was old enough to know that stealing and lying are always wrong. We spanked him, and we cried. We held him, and we cried. We made him return the toy to the friend and confess to him—and we cried. It was one of the toughest things we have ever done. Yet it was right, and we are glad we did it. God was pleased, and a piece of the foundation was placed securely in a little boy's life.

An important aspect of walking uprightly is righting wrongs. This involves confessing the sin to God (because all sin is ultimately against God), confessing the sin to the person sinned against, and seeking that person's forgiveness.

We taught our boys to practice the Twelve Golden Words approach to righting wrongs: "I was wrong," "I am sorry," "Please forgive me," and "I love you."

4. Guide them to humility.

> *Humility is the fear of the Lord;*
> *its wages are riches and honor and life.*
> PROVERBS 22:4 NIV

Fearing God is linked with humility. Humility comes from *highly esteeming God*. The Bible doesn't tell us to seek *self*-esteem, but good self-esteem results when we give God his rightful glory and honor. If we esteem God highly, as He deserves, and then realize that this awesome, lofty God esteems and loves us, then we will have true self-esteem.

Humility is the result of *viewing ourselves accurately*—not thinking too highly of ourselves *or* too lowly. It is seeing ourselves as God sees us.

Humility comes when we *make God central* in our lives. We must not treat our kids as the center of the universe. Only God deserves such distinction. We do our kids a great disservice by putting them in the place of God, because it is a position they cannot possibly fill. They will become self-centered, and a self-centered life will always become a life of disappointment.

Humility is linked with *an interest in others*. Not only is self-centeredness unattractive, but it is also in opposition to the fear of the Lord. We must help our kids realize that there is a whole world of people beyond themselves. When I was a boy, my mother regularly took me to visit shut-ins, people in nursing homes, and others in need of encouragement. I am very grateful for her effort at helping me develop an interest in others.

5. Teach them to respect authority.

God is the ultimate authority. Therefore, all rebellion is ultimately against God. If I cannot get my children to respect and obey *me*, whom they can see, then they will struggle to respect and obey *God*, whom they cannot see.

Authority is God-ordained. We need to help our children respect all levels of human authority, including parental, civic, vocational, and spiritual authorities. If my kids can learn to respect imperfect human authority, they will find it easier to respect perfect divine authority. There is an unmistakable link between our attitude toward divine authority and our attitude toward all authority.

Children tend to respect authority as long as it is respectable. Once they lose respect for authority, it is difficult to regain. Start early by being respectful and respectable. Model respect for authority in your words and deeds. Do not allow your children to show disrespect. Defiant toddlers can become delinquent teenagers.

The Benefits of Fearing the Lord

I realize that the notion of fearing God is not popular in our culture and will not necessarily be a popular view with your children's peers. Yet a lack of popularity does not make the fear of the Lord any less necessary or beneficial. I challenge and encourage you to lay this vital foundation in the lives of your children. If you do, they will reap significant benefits:

1. Wisdom

> *The fear of the Lord is the beginning of* wisdom.
> PROVERBS 9:10 (EMPHASIS ADDED)

2. Strong confidence and safety

> *In the fear of the Lord one has* strong confidence,
> *and his children will have a refuge.*
> PROVERBS 14:26 (EMPHASIS ADDED)

3. Life

> *The fear of the Lord is a* fountain of life,
> *that one may turn away from the snares of death.*
> PROVERBS 14:27 (EMPHASIS ADDED)

4. A peace that money can't buy

> Better is a little with the fear of the Lord
> than great treasure and trouble with it.
> PROVERBS 15:16

5. Satisfaction

> The fear of the Lord leads to life,
> and he who has it will abide in satisfaction.
> PROVERBS 19:23 NKJV (EMPHASIS ADDED)

6. Happiness

> Happy is the man who is always reverent,
> but he who hardens his heart will fall into calamity.
> PROVERBS 28:14 NKJV (EMPHASIS ADDED)

A Look in the Mirror

Evaluate your laying of a proper foundation by answering the following questions:

1. Do I take God seriously? How would my children know?

2. What am I doing to help my children take God's Word seriously? Do they see me reading it? Do I read it to them? Do we talk about it? Do we make efforts to apply it?

3. Have my children come to know the Lord as their personal Savior? What am I doing to help them grow in their relationship with Him? Am I growing in my relationship with Him?

4. What efforts am I making to help my children walk uprightly? Have I taught them how to properly right wrongs?

5. What do I do to help them see that God is the center of the universe?

6. Do I respect those in authority over me? Am I modeling respect for authority?

4 Set a Good Example

One hot summer day, as I prepared to mow the lawn, I noticed that my preschool-age sons, Daniel and Andrew, were imitating my every move. When I filled the mower with gas, they both pretended to pour gas into their little red plastic mowers. When I pulled the cord to start my mower, they pulled their pretend cords to start theirs. When I pushed my mower out into the grass, they pushed their little red mowers into the grass. When I turned at the end of the yard, they turned at the end of the yard. When I stopped the mower to wipe the sweat off my forehead, they both stopped to wipe the sweat off their foreheads. It was all very cute.

Especially at certain ages, children love to imitate their parents. Sometimes it is endearing and rewarding; other times it can be embarrassing. On that particular summer day, I felt a rush of pride as my sons imitated my every move—that is, until they saw me grumble and kick my mower because it wouldn't restart and they both grumbled and kicked their little plastic mowers.

Rest assured, your children will imitate your good traits, but they will tend to imitate your negative traits twice as easily and often. Therefore, it is essential to set the right example. I am not talking about being perfect, but I am talking about being on the right path (the path of wisdom) and making progress.

Children often learn much more from our example than from our lectures. Never underestimate the power of your example to influence your children.

Secret #4
Set a good example.

Get Plastered

Ben Franklin, a gifted inventor, understood the power of an example to teach and train others. When he inadvertently discovered that raw gypsum—called land plaster in his day—made great fertilizer, he told his neighbors about his discovery. When they refused to listen to him or to try his suggestion, he decided to stop telling and start showing.

One moonlit night, he slipped out to the edge of town to a field that sat along a well-traveled road. Taking a supply of gypsum, he wrote a message in the grass: "This field was plastered."

Of course, the plaster fertilized part of the field grew faster, stronger, and brighter than the rest. Soon the field had its message blazing out in bright green for all to see.

Franklin did not need to say anything more to his neighbors

about the value of plaster as a fertilizer. They got the message through his example, not his words. The evident growth and the bright green letters did the teaching.

"You Cannot Impart What You Do Not Possess"

Several years ago, Dr. Howard Hendricks of Dallas Seminary spoke at our church. Several times during his message on the family he repeated a simple refrain: "You cannot impart what you do not possess." As parents, our goal is to impart wisdom to our children. But that will be impossible if we do not possess wisdom ourselves.

Proverbs 13:20 says, "Whoever walks with the wise becomes wise." This universal principle includes the parent-child relationship. If we want our children to be wise, we must start by being wise ourselves. The more we walk in wisdom as parents, the easier it will be for our children to walk in wisdom by following our example.

I have found that some aspects of wisdom have been easier for me to develop than others—the ones that my parents modeled most clearly for me.

Take Inventory

Proverbs paints a panoramic portrait of the wise person in various life situations. In the rest of this chapter, we will look at six key characteristics of a wise person. Then we will evaluate ourselves to discover which aspects of wisdom we possess. The goal is to have a good understanding of what it means to be wise and how we measure up, so that we can build on our strengths and work on our weaknesses.

In the following sections, read the questions, verses, and explanations carefully, and then evaluate yourself on a scale from 1 ("I need major help here") to 5 ("I have this one down"). Remember, it takes wise parents to produce wise children.

The Wise Pursue Wisdom with Devotion and Determination

As a pastor for several decades, I have observed hundreds of different Christians of different ages, backgrounds, personalities, and abilities. The common denominator of spiritual success is whether they become devoted, determined pursuers of wisdom in God's Word. Those who read and study the Word regularly keep going on the path of wisdom. Those who do not. . .well, they do not.

My son, if you receive my words and treasure up my commandments with you, making your ear attentive to wisdom and inclining your heart to understanding; yes, if you call out for insight and raise your voice for understanding, if you seek it like silver and search for it as for hidden treasures, then you will understand the fear of the Lord and find the knowledge of God. For the Lord gives wisdom; from his mouth come knowledge and understanding.

PROVERBS 2:1–6

Hear instruction and be wise, and do not neglect it. Blessed is the one who listens to me, watching daily at my gates, waiting beside my doors.

PROVERBS 8:33–34

As we read these words from Solomon, we discover four key truths:

- Wisdom comes from God (2:6).

- God's wisdom is revealed primarily in His Word (2:1, 6).

- God's Word gives wisdom to those who pursue it with devotion and determination (2:1–4).

- We need a regular (daily) infusion of wisdom in order to stay on the right path (8:33).

As someone once observed, "It doesn't matter how much money you have, everyone has to purchase wisdom on the installment plan."

I have found that those who regularly pursue wisdom in God's Word have certain common characteristics:

• They have a regular *time* for Bible study (first thing in the morning, at lunch, or before bed).

• They have a regular *amount of time* for the Word (fifteen minutes daily or one hour three evenings a week).

• They have a usual *place* for study (a desk, favorite chair, the kitchen table, or in bed).

• They have a general *plan* for Bible reading and study. (I suggest you start by reading one chapter of Proverbs each day—the thirty-one chapters conveniently align with the days of the month.)

My regular time for Bible reading is_____

My amount of time is_____

My favorite place is_____

My plan for Bible reading is_____

Rate your pursuit of wisdom.

1   2   3   4   5

The Wise Work with Initiative, Foresight, and Diligence

My father was an excellent worker. He also wisely instilled a work ethic into my life at a young age. When I was nine, for example, he signed me up for a paper route. I will never forget going downtown to pick up my collection bag, route book, and delivery bag. I had twenty-five customers every afternoon and nearly one hundred for the large Sunday morning edition.

Dad set a great example of hard work by getting me up early every Sunday to stuff and deliver the paper. He helped me load the massive Sunday edition into the trunk of his Toyota and drove me around my route—delivering nearly half of those large papers himself. He taught me how to work *by working with me*. I will always be indebted to him for developing my character in this way.

He also taught me that no matter how tired I was or how bad the weather, people were depending on me to bring their newspaper. He refused to let me make excuses.

It's easy to get into the habit of making excuses to cover our laziness. Solomon refers to the lazy man as a sluggard. He writes,

"The sluggard says, 'There is a lion outside! I shall be killed in the streets!'" (Proverbs 22:13).

Making excuses starts young. When my son Andrew was three, I asked him to stop running around and to pick up his toys.

"I can't," he said, "I'm too tired."

"You can't be tired; you were just running all over the house."

"Well, then," he grimaced, "my tummy hurts."

"Your tummy doesn't hurt," I said. "Now pick up your toys."

"Oh, Daddy, I can't," he sighed as he looked up at me. "I'm just a little boy."

The wise learn not to make excuses. They work hard with initiative, foresight, and diligence. Note what Solomon says about the wise work ethic of the ant compared with the excuses of the lazy fool:

> *You lazy fool, look at an ant. Watch it closely; let it teach you a thing or two. Nobody has to tell it what to do. All summer it stores up food; at harvest it stockpiles provisions. So how long are you going to laze around doing nothing? How long before you get out of bed? A nap here, a nap there, a day off here, a day off there, sit back, take it easy— do you know what comes next? Just this: You can look forward to a dirt-poor life, poverty your permanent houseguest!*
>
> PROVERBS 6:6–11 MSG

Note that the ant, unlike the lazy fool, has the initiative to start work without the need of a supervisor. Also, the ant displays foresight by storing winter provisions during the summer, unlike the lazy sluggard, who just sleeps.

Look in the mirror. Think about your work habits at home and on the job, if applicable. Would your mate or boss say that you work with initiative, foresight, and diligence? Will your children do well in life if they imitate your work ethic?

Rate your initiative, foresight, and diligence.

1   2   3   4   5

The Wise Are Teachable

A man who occasionally came to our church always made a point of saying that he didn't need anyone telling him how to run his life. He knew what was best for him, and he was not about to listen to anyone else. Interestingly, as his children grew up, this same man lamented that they never listened to him or took his advice. Small wonder! They had learned that attitude from him.

If your children are unteachable, did they learn it from you? If you don't accept advice or criticism well, can you really expect your kids to do otherwise? If you gripe about authority or constantly criticize your boss, you are teaching your children to respond to authority in the same manner.

The wise continue to learn throughout their lives. My parents were still sharp, interesting, and wise in their seventies because they continued taking college courses and learning new skills throughout their adult lives.

The wisdom of being teachable is an oft-repeated theme in Proverbs (see 9:8–9; 10:8; 10:14; 12:15; 13:1; 15:31; 17:10; 19:20; 21:11; 24:6; 26:12). Note that the primary difference between the foolish and the wise is how they respond to opportunities to learn.

Do not reprove a scoffer, or he will hate you; reprove a wise man, and he will love you. Give instruction to a wise man, and he will be still wiser; teach a righteous man, and he will increase in learning.

PROVERBS 9:8–9

The way of a fool is right in his own eyes, but a wise man listens to advice.

PROVERBS 12:15

A wise son hears his father's instruction, but a scoffer does not listen to rebuke.

PROVERBS 13:1

Listen to advice and accept instruction,
that you may gain wisdom in the future.
PROVERBS 19:20

Do you see a man who is wise in his own eyes?
There is more hope for a fool than for him.
PROVERBS 26:12

Rate your teachability.
1   2   3   4   5

The Wise Flee from Evil

A wise man fears and departs from evil,
but a fool rages and is self-confident.
PROVERBS 14:16 NKJV

The wise see danger, respect the consequences, and avoid evil. A positive example of this aspect of wisdom is Joseph (Genesis 39:1–12). His master's wife repeatedly tempted him to have sex with her. This was no small temptation. He was a young man. She was a powerful woman who could make his life easier. No one was around or would ever need to know. Her requests were repeated frequently.

Yet Joseph "feared and departed from evil." He did not fear his master, Potiphar. He feared God. He literally ran from Potiphar's wife, explaining, "How can I do such an evil thing and sin against God?"

A negative example of the fool who failed to act wisely is Samson (Judges 16). Thinking he was invincible, he walked into an evil relationship with Delilah. Samson had no fear of God, nor did he fear evil or its consequences. As a result, he lost his hair, his strength, his freedom, his eyes, his testimony, his dignity, and his life.

Look in the mirror. Do you toy with evil or shun it? Have you learned to depart from evil actions, thoughts, and attitudes? We cannot flirt with evil and then expect our children to flee from it.

Rate your commitment to flee from evil.

1 2 3 4 5

The Wise Control Their Finances

Financial self-discipline is another characteristic of the wise (Proverbs 21:5; 27:23–24), whereas fools spend indiscriminately (Proverbs 21:20). The issue is not how much you earn. It is what you do with what you earn.

My father developed wisdom in my life by teaching me how

to handle money. Because of his example, I control my money instead of it controlling me.

My father taught me how to *earn* money by helping me with my paper route. He taught me how to *save* money by opening a savings account for me and showing me how to use it. He taught me that interest—which I viewed as free money—was only available to the savers, not the wasters.

He taught me to *give* money by his marvelous example of generosity. Generous giving is another characteristic of the wise (Proverbs 3:9–10). And he taught me how to *budget* money by showing me how he recorded his expenditures on a pad on his dresser every night after work. He spent one day a month, often on a Saturday afternoon as he watched a football game, balancing his checkbook and preparing the next month's budget.

Rate your financial self-discipline.

1   2   3   4   5

The Wise Control Their Temper

Wise people avoid angry outbursts and impulsive reactions.

Scoffers set a city aflame,
but the wise turn away wrath.
Proverbs 29:8

I once heard someone refer to displays of anger as "the weak person's imitation of strength." Sadly, spouses and parents often use anger to get their way. They know if they blow up, their mate or children will back down. Unfortunately, this approach produces a lot of resentment. Wise people turn away from angry outbursts.

A fool gives full vent to his spirit,
but a wise man quietly holds it back.
PROVERBS 29:11

Being reactive is easy. The problem is that our first reaction is usually not good. Ben Franklin said, "Anger is never without a reason, but seldom with a good one." Remember, an angry argument can be defined as "an activity during which people exchange their ignorance."

The wise maintain their self-control. They know when to hold back and how to calm the storm. Likewise, a wise parent learns how to remain cool, calm, and collected. Ultimately, this is the most effective approach. As Proverbs 15:1 says, "A soft answer turns away wrath, but a harsh word stirs up anger."

One study revealed that nearly 90 percent of relational friction is caused by *tone of voice*. When we speak, our words convey your thoughts, but our tone conveys our mood. Our tone is what people pick up on, not our words.

Anger and wisdom do not mix. In the words of a Chinese proverb, "When anger comes, then wisdom goes."

Rate your control of your temper.

1   2   3   4   5

A Look in the Mirror

Mirrors are marvelous tools of self-evaluation. On the one hand, we love them because we are fascinated at looking at ourselves. On the other hand, we hate them because they show every bruise, bump, and blemish.

The epistle of James speaks often of wisdom (1:5; 3:13–17), directly and practically pushing us to apply the Word of God to our lives. At one point, James refers to God's Word as a spiritual mirror that reveals our need to get back on the path of wisdom:

> *Don't fool yourself into thinking that you are a listener when you are anything but, letting the Word go in one ear and out the other. Act on what you hear! Those who hear and don't act are like those who glance in the mirror, walk away, and two minutes later have no idea who they are, what they look like. But whoever catches a glimpse of the revealed counsel of God—*

> *the free life!—even out of the corner of his eye, and sticks with it,*
> *is no distracted scatterbrain but a man or woman of action.*
> *That person will find delight and affirmation in the action.*
>
> JAMES 1:22–25 MSG

The wise evaluate their behavior and discern their way (Proverbs 14:8). When you hold up the mirror of God's Word to your life, what do you see? Where do you need to take action in order to become a wise person capable of setting a right example for your children?

As you grow in and display wisdom, you will set the pace for your children.

5 Understand the Problem

When our boys were still quite young, we watched a movie together as a family about Tom Sawyer and Huck Finn. Later that night, as the boys were in the bathtub, I left the room for a minute to answer the phone. When I returned, I found them carrying on riotously—laughing, yelling, and pouring water on each other from the lids of the bubble bath.

I squared my shoulders and in my best angry dad voice asked, "What on earth are you guys doing?"

"We're drunk," they laughed with convincingly slurred speech. "Drunker than skunks," they giggled.

"Drunk?" I gasped. "Where did you learn about drinking?"

"From the Tom Sawyer movie," they answered with complete innocence.

"Remember Huck's dad?" Daniel replied. "He was drunk from drinking whiskey."

"Drunker than a skunk," Andrew chimed in.

I could not believe it. Here we had watched a nice, family-oriented movie, and what had they learned? Out of a two-hour movie, they picked up on a tiny, two-minute scene where Huck's dad got drunk! Someone in the scene laughed and said that he was "drunker than a skunk." And it was the only thing my boys remembered!

The next night we were seated around the table for dinner. One-year-old Luke grabbed a piece of pizza from Andrew's plate and quickly stuffed part of it into his mouth. Andrew wanted the rest of it back, but Luke snatched it and yelled, "Mine." He would not give it up, but kept yelling, "Mine."

The following week, as we sat around the table and said a prayer of thanks for the meal, I heard something whiz by my head. I opened my eyes to see food flying across the table as the boys launched into a full-fledged food fight. They were squealing in delight as freshly splattered food ran down their faces. It took a while to get them calmed down and the food cleaned up.

Finally, Cathy asked, "What is wrong with these kids?"

After a few moments of deep contemplation, a lightbulb appeared over my head. I looked at my wife and the boys and with grave insight responded, "Theologically speaking, the problem is that they are sinners."

The Biggest Problem Children Are Facing Today

What do you think is the biggest problem facing children today? As a parent, what should you fear the most? What one thing should we combat with our greatest efforts? I compiled a list from various media reports that mentioned serious problems facing children today. Which do you see as the most significant?

→ Poverty?

→ Global warming?

→ Pollution?

→ Secular education?

→ Peer pressure?

→ Government intervention?

→ Substance abuse?

→ Materialism?

→ Physical abuse?

→ Secular humanism?

→ Violence?

→ Television?

→ Crime?

→ Teen pregnancy?

→ Gangs?

→ Racism?

→ Ungodly music and movies?

→ Sexually transmitted diseases?

→ Suicide?

→ Teenage runaways?

→ The Internet?

→ Sexual abuse?

Did you find it hard to pick just one? Which one do you think the Bible would say is your child's biggest problem?

The answer found in the book of Proverbs is not on the list. It is not recognized by many so-called experts on parenting and children, yet it is very real and in many ways is foundational to the other problems on the list. It must be understood and dealt with if our children are going to walk in wisdom and avoid the pain caused by the other items on the list.

Your Child's Biggest Problem

So what is the biggest problem our children face? According to Proverbs, it is *foolishness*, or *folly*.

> *Folly is bound up in the heart of a child,*
> *but the rod of discipline drives it far from him.*
> PROVERBS 22:15

Secret #5
Overcome your child's inner foolishness.

Three False Notions about Folly

To detect folly and drive it far from our children's hearts, we must first understand what it is and why it is such a problem. It is helpful to note three qualities that do not constitute foolishness.

Folly is not mental incapacity. Someone can have a low IQ or be mentally slow without being *foolish*. On the other hand, one can have a high IQ and a very sharp mind and yet be a classic fool.

Folly is not normal immaturity. It takes time for infants to develop into children and for children to develop into mature adults. The Bible doesn't expect a three-year-old to act like a thirty-year-old. Children can giggle, wiggle, cry easily, and spill their milk without being foolish. On the other hand, a person might seem to epitomize dignity and yet have a heart of folly.

Folly is not normal curiosity. There is nothing wrong with normal curiosity. God made children inquisitive on purpose. Curiosity fuels discovery, and discovery produces learning. My children have always asked a steady barrage of questions. This is how they learn. Curiosity is a vital part of a child's nature, which a skillful parent uses to direct the child to God and His way of wisdom.

The Nature of Foolishness or Folly

If folly is not mental incapability, natural immaturity, or normal curiosity, what is it? Three Hebrew words are used for "foolishness" in Proverbs. The word used most often, *kesil* (fifty times), describes a state of dullness and obstinacy. The foolish person has chosen to be this way. Fools have no appetite for wisdom because they think they don't need it. The root problem is spiritual, not mental. They reject God's authority and thus are a great danger to themselves and others.

Evil, the second most often-used word for folly (nineteen times), suggests stupidity and stubbornness. The person with this nature is "loud and quarrelsome, undisciplined and unteachable."

The last word, *nabal* (three times), describes a mind and heart that is closed to God and reason. Fools choose not to be open to God's work in their lives.

Combining these terms, we could define foolishness as "an inner attitude or spiritual disposition that stubbornly chooses to close one's mind to God, authority, reproof, self-discipline, and wisdom." More simply, it is "a natural bent to leave God out and to avoid the way of wisdom." Most simply, folly is the opposite of wisdom. It is a manifestation of what the New Testament calls "the old nature."

Folly Is an Inside Job

Children are born with a foolish, sinful nature. Any parent will tell you they don't have to teach their children to do wrong.

The kids figure it out well enough on their own. Instead, parents have to teach their children to do right.

We rarely left our boys with babysitters, because we couldn't tell them everything *not to do*. Inevitably, we would come home to a shell-shocked babysitter and three "innocent" little boys who would say, "But you didn't say we couldn't climb on the roof" or "You didn't say not to shoot the neighbor with a BB gun."

Folly reflects the sinful nature of children. They have a natural inner bent to avoid wisdom and pursue folly.

The Four Perils of Folly

What makes folly so dangerous that it must be forcibly removed from our children's hearts? Once folly is entrenched, it is not easily removed. Left unchecked, folly will cause a child to become what Proverbs refers to as a *fool*.

> *Though you grind a fool in a mortar, grinding them like grain with a pestle, you will not remove their folly from them.*
> PROVERBS 27:22 NIV

Foolishness is the enemy of wisdom. Just as darkness opposes light and evil opposes good, so does folly oppose wisdom. It is the antithesis of all we hope our children will become.

With wisdom, a child can overcome temptation and walk uprightly. Without wisdom, the lust of the eye and the pride of life will drag a child down. Think of the Bible hero Daniel. He was placed in the ungodly world of Babylon as a teenager, surrounded by false religion, temptation, and wickedness. Yet because he had learned to walk in wisdom as a child, he did not allow the surrounding culture to influence him. Instead, he influenced the culture for God.

Fools cause tremendous emotional pain for their parents. Fools are listed in Proverbs as the ones who break their parents' hearts.

> *A wise son brings joy to his father,*
> *but a foolish son brings grief to his mother.*
> PROVERBS 10:1 NIV

> *To have a fool for a child brings grief;*
> *there is no joy for the parent of a godless fool.*
> PROVERBS 17:21 NIV

> *A foolish son is a grief to his father*
> *and bitterness to her who bore him.*
> PROVERBS 17:25

Grief, sorrow, and bitterness are unpleasant consequences. Sadly, many parents in our culture have raised children who have become foolish adults, and the parents now feel the pain. Syndicated columnist Ann Landers surveyed parents, asking them to share their feelings about having children. Seventy percent of respondents said, in effect, "If I had it to do over again, I would not have any children."

When children are allowed to keep their inner bent of folly, they may eventually despise their parents. Foolishness can grow into a sense of disrespect for parents, which can manifest as anything from apathy to neglect to outright violence.

A foolish child is a father's ruin.
PROVERBS 19:13 NIV

The word *ruin* speaks to the repeated embarrassments and destructive results inflicted by a fool upon his or her parents. It is sad to see parents who were unwilling or unable to drive folly from their children's hearts when they were small now have to deal with the ongoing effects of their children's foolishness as they become adults.

One Christian couple, in an effort to cover up the illegitimacy of a child produced by their foolish son, tried raising their granddaughter as their daughter. Sadly, she turned out to be a fool as well. She produced an illegitimate child of her own, repeatedly ran away from home, became involved in drugs, and was in trouble with the police—all before her sixteenth birthday. This nearly ruined her grandparents' marriage, their walk with God, and their relationship with their other children.

Fools hurt other people. It's not easy to accept that if my child becomes a fool, I am partly responsible for the pain he or she inflicts on others. Everyone who gets involved with a fool is negatively affected, including spouses, children, friends, and coworkers.

> *A companion of fools suffers harm.*
> PROVERBS 13:20 NIV

> *Stay away from a fool.*
> PROVERBS 14:7 NIV

> *Better to meet a bear robbed of her cubs than a fool bent on folly.*
> PROVERBS 17:12

> *The wise woman builds her house, but with her own hands the foolish one tears hers down.*
> PROVERBS 14:1 NIV

Fools frustrate all who depend on them. Too often they take others to destruction with them.

Sadly, as a pastor, I have too often witnessed the heartache and pain inflicted by fools on their families. Irresponsibility, poor judgment, laziness, slander, impulsiveness, quarreling, and anger characterize the home life of a fool.

Fools destroy themselves. One who refuses the way of wisdom refuses the way of life and chooses instead the way of destruction.

> *The waywardness of the simple will kill them,*
> *and the complacency of fools will destroy them.*
> PROVERBS 1:32 NIV

> *A chattering fool comes to ruin.*
> PROVERBS 10:8 NIV

> *Fools die for lack of sense.*
> PROVERBS 10:21 NIV

> *A person's own folly leads to their ruin.*
> PROVERBS 19:3 NIV

Destruction, ruin, and death are the results of folly—whether it is financial, through waste, haste, or poor decision-making;

physical, such as a sexually transmitted disease, drug addiction, suicide, or imprisonment; or relational, through calamity, chaos, regret, and remorse. Regardless of form, a fool's destruction is ultimately spiritual. Wanting nothing to do with God on earth, the fool is separated from Him throughout eternity.

The Heart of Folly

Folly has a rotten root, so it will always bear ugly fruit. This root is revealed in the Psalms, where the heart of the fool is exposed.

> *The fool says in his heart, "There is no God."*
> PSALMS 14:1; 53:1

The heart of folly is a *denial of God*. It can range from mere apathy to outright refusal to acknowledge God's existence. Folly negates God's perspective and ignores His wisdom. It shuns His help, resists His will, and demeans His Word.

Folly is another word for *practical atheism*—living as if God does not exist—and *practical materialism*, living as if wealth and possessions are all that matter. It is the driving force behind *practical humanism*—living as if man, not God, is central in the universe.

But if God is central to the universe, as the Bible teaches, and all good comes from God, then folly will deprive the fool of true, eternal, ultimate good. No God, no good.

What Does Folly Look Like?

Just as medical doctors use symptoms to diagnose disease, wise parents will know the symptoms of folly so they can help their children avoid its dangerous consequences. Folly has five principal symptoms:

1. Pride and self-centeredness
Because fools refuse to be God-centered, they exalt and trust themselves.

> *Those who trust in themselves are fools.*
> PROVERBS 28:26 NIV

> *Do you see a person wise in their own eyes?*
> *There is more hope for a fool than for them.*
> PROVERBS 26:12 NIV

Self-centeredness is the most obvious manifestation of folly. Fools act as if the world revolves around them instead of around God and His wisdom.

As parents, we must start early in teaching our children about God. We must help them learn to think of others and not just of themselves. The saddest people I know are not the ones with the most problems but the ones who are the most self-centered.

I am the third of three children in my family. As the baby, I tended to be self-centered. My mother helped me to broaden my perspective by taking me with her to visit shut-ins and people in nursing homes, where I learned to consider the needs of others. Though I balked at the time, I am now thankful for her wisdom in stretching my world and taking my focus off of me.

2. An unteachable spirit

Because fools have such an inflated opinion of themselves, they don't want to learn from others; they think they already know everything. As a result, fools resist God's authority and instruction. They don't want to *hear* what He says because they don't want to *do* what He says. Fools hate the thought of being told what to do.

> *The fear of the Lord is the beginning of knowledge,*
> but fools despise wisdom and instruction.
> PROVERBS 1:7 NIV (EMPHASIS ADDED)

A man's own folly ruins his life,
yet his heart rages against the Lord.
Proverbs 19:3

Fools reject the advice and authority of their parents and others. Unlike the wise, they don't take criticism well. In fact, they hate anyone who tries to correct them (Proverbs 9:7–8; 12:15; 15:5; 23:9).

Fools do not pursue wisdom. They see no need to read the Bible. They feel no compulsion to listen to wise teaching. Instead, they satisfy themselves with their own opinions and ideas (Proverbs 1:22; 17:16; 18:2).

Fools don't learn from their mistakes. The tragedy of folly is that it blinds a fool to his or her blunders, blind spots, and weaknesses. Consequently, the fool often goes on to even greater foolishness (Proverbs 17:10; 26:11).

3. A lack of dependability

Fools refuse to accept responsibility. They cannot be counted on and should not be trusted. They are too unreliable and irresponsible to reach their potential.

Sending a message by the hands of a fool is
like cutting off one's feet or drinking poison.
Proverbs 26:6 NIV

> *Like the useless legs of one who is lame is a proverb*
> *in the mouth of a fool. . . . Like a thornbush in a*
> *drunkard's hand is a proverb in the mouth of a fool.*
> PROVERBS 26:7, 9 NIV

> *Like snow in summer or rain in harvest,*
> *honor is not fitting for a fool.*
> PROVERBS 26:1 NIV

> *Whoever brings ruin on their family will inherit only wind,*
> *and the fool will be servant to the wise.*
> PROVERBS 11:29 NIV

4. A lack of discipline

Fools lack self-control and are undisciplined in every area of life.

Fools lack self-control in their use of money. By violating the basic principles of sound money management, fools bring trouble on themselves. They do not avoid debt, keep records, plan expenditures, save and invest wisely, avoid hasty spending, practice contentment, or honor God with their money (Proverbs 3:9–10; 15:16–17; 21:5, 20; 22:7; 27:23–24).

Fools lack self-control in their speech. They talk much and say little. The more they talk, the more trouble they get into. A fool's words are frequent, many, hasty, and unproductive (Proverbs 12:23; 14:3; 15:2; 17:28; 18:6–7, 13; 29:20).

Fools lack self-discipline in their emotions. They cannot control their temper. They are hotheaded, quarrelsome, reckless, and easily irritated (Proverbs 12:16; 14:16–17, 29; 20:3; 29:9, 11).

5. Ungodliness

Fools run from God toward sin. They do not view sin as something to be avoided. To a fool, sin is something to dabble with, play with, enjoy, and pursue. Such ungodly complacency will certainly lead to calamity.

> *Fools mock at making amends for sin.*
> PROVERBS 14:9 NIV

> *A fool finds pleasure in wicked schemes.*
> PROVERBS 10:23 NIV

> *The complacency of fools will destroy them.*
> PROVERBS 1:32 NIV

A Look in the Mirror

Now that you understand the problem of folly, there are three things you should do:

1. *Honestly evaluate your children.* Determine which of the symptoms of folly are most prevalent and which are not. Thank God for the areas of wisdom and build on them. Pray, and begin working on the areas of folly before they become entrenched. Answer the following questions:

• How many symptoms of folly do you see in your children? Are your children self-centered? Do their conversations revolve around themselves and their activities? How are you helping them see God as central? How are you stretching their world to get their eyes off of themselves? How can your family become more "others" oriented?

• How teachable are your children? How often do they have to be told or shown something? Do they admit mistakes? Do they work to overcome weaknesses? Do they pursue wisdom? Are they readers? Do they listen to sound teaching?

• How responsible are your children? Depending on their ages, do they perform household chores? Can they be trusted? Do they tell the truth? Are they faithful with a little responsibility and thus deserve more?

• Have your children learned self-control? Do they control their time and money? Are they learning to handle money wisely? Do they control their speech? Have they developed the ability to remain emotionally under control?

2. *Sincerely examine yourself.* Which characteristics of folly are your biggest struggles? Are you practicing and modeling wisdom? Pray and ask God to help rid your life of folly.

3. *Candidly explore your parenting strategy and techniques.* If you see a lot of folly in your children, you may need to develop some new strategies for correcting the problem. The next several chapters will teach you some important tools.

6   Correct the Behavior

When it comes to home repairs, I have problems. If I know what to do, I don't have the right tool. If I have the right tool, I either don't how to use it or can't find it. If I know what to do, have the right tool—in hand—and know how to use it, the job will still take all day and require several trips to the hardware store.

Over the years, however, my skills have improved, and I have acquired an impressive array of tools. But I still need to learn how to use them more effectively.

The Tools of Parenting

The rod and reproof give wisdom, but a child left to himself brings shame to his mother.
PROVERBS 29:15

Proverbs gives three primary tools for wise parents to use to correct their children's behavior and help them develop wisdom: the *rod* of discipline, the *reproof* of instruction, and the *refusal* to leave children to themselves; that is, *involvement* in their lives.

In later chapters, we will discuss the tools of *reproof* and *personal involvement.* For the rest of this chapter, we will discuss the tool of *discipline.*

The Importance of Discipline

Six of the seven directives given to parents in Proverbs deal with the tool of discipline (13:24; 19:18; 22:15; 23:13–14; 29:15, 17). In the seventh—"training children in the way they should go" (22:6)—the role of discipline is implied. According to Proverbs, the tool of discipline is essential for raising wise kids. We cannot do the job without it.

Secret #6
Correct the problem of foolishness with loving discipline.

Five Reasons Parents Must Use the Tool of Discipline

1. Without discipline, foolishness cannot be removed from a child.

> *Folly is bound up in the heart of a child,*
> *but the rod of discipline will drive it far away.*
> PROVERBS 22:15 NIV

Do not withhold discipline from a child;
if you punish them with a rod, they will not die.
Punish them with the rod and save them from death.
PROVERBS 23:13–14 NIV

Discipline your children, for in that there is hope;
do not be a willing party to their death.
PROVERBS 19:18 NIV

Several years ago, we moved to a new house. The previous owners had liked to garden and had many plants. We moved in at the beginning of spring, just as all the plants began to reawaken. Though I considered myself a fairly effective gardener, I encountered problems in my new yard: I couldn't distinguish between the weeds and the flowers. To determine what to pull and what to leave, I developed a simple strategy: pull the ones that grew the fastest and spread out most quickly. (They must be the weeds.) The ones I needed to nurse along had to be the flowers.

Foolishness is like a weed in our character. It plants itself easily, grows quickly, and tries to choke out positive character qualities before they can get firmly established. We must weed out foolishness before it can develop, or it will soon get out of hand. We must pull it out at the roots, or it will come back stronger.

Weeding out foolishness requires diligence and persistence. Early and often it must be dug up, cut off, and choked off from a child's life. If not, it will soon take over your child's character and be very difficult to remove.

As Dr. Albert Siegel has keenly observed, "When it comes to rearing children, every society is only twenty years away from barbarism. Twenty years is all we have to accomplish the task of civilizing the infants who are born into our midst each year."[1] Barbarians are uncivilized savages. They are selfish brutes, insensitive to others and lacking in self-control. No doubt you have observed children who have passed through the brat stage and are well on their way to barbarism. Without discipline, foolishness cannot be removed.

2. Without discipline, your children will not acquire wisdom.

> *A rod and a reprimand impart wisdom.*
> PROVERBS 29:15 NIV

> *Whoever heeds life-giving correction will be at home among the wise.*
> *Those who disregard discipline despise themselves,*
> *but the one who heeds correction gains understanding.*
> PROVERBS 15:31–32 NIV

Discipline not only removes the weed of folly but it also imparts the flower of wisdom. It plants, waters, and fertilizes wisdom in a child's life.

Another way to view discipline is as a lane marker on the way to wisdom. It indicates the path, defines the boundaries, and keeps the child on the right road.

3. Without discipline, your children won't feel loved.

> *Whoever spares the rod hates their children, but the one who loves their children is careful to discipline them.*
> PROVERBS 13:24 NIV

> *My son, do not despise the Lord's discipline, and do not resent his rebuke, because the Lord disciplines those he loves, as a father the son he delights in.*
> PROVERBS 3:11–12 NIV

Some wrongly view discipline as a harsh, abusive act. This could not be further from the truth. Genuine discipline, given to impart wisdom, is the clearest expression of parental love described in the Bible. I have heard parents say that they love their children too much to discipline them. Such a notion is mistaken and illogical. Consider the facts. First, folly is dangerous. It must be removed.

It is not removed without discipline.

Second, wisdom is the desired goal. It is elusive and must be acquired. Discipline is a necessary tool for imparting wisdom.

Third, failing to use discipline means failure to remove folly and failure to impart wisdom. Therefore, neglecting to use discipline is unloving.

The reason we disciplined our boys was precisely because we *loved* them. If we didn't love them, we wouldn't have gone through the hassle of disciplining them. We wouldn't have cared if they played in the street or touched a hot stove. We would have said, "Go ahead, express yourselves. Be creative, and leave us alone." If they wanted to get in a car with a stranger, use drugs, vandalize the community, or be lazy slobs, so be it.

But we *did* care. We loved them intensely. We were highly committed to them. We cared about their well-being. We felt responsible for them. We disciplined them because they were ours and we loved them.

The same was not true with the neighbors' kids. Although we did love them, our love for them was not nearly the same. Our level of commitment, concern, and responsibility was not as intense, because they weren't ours. I spanked my children when they needed it, but I never spanked the neighbors' children— although I wanted to on occasion. Why didn't I discipline the neighbors' kids? Because they weren't mine.

Parents who love their children will discipline them. That is one way I know that I am a child of God: I cannot sin and get away with it. My heavenly Father loves me enough to rebuke me me when I need it. He uses discipline to guide me back into the way of wisdom (Proverbs 3:11–12; Hebrews 12:5–6).

Love means doing what is best for your children. If you love them, you will discipline them.

4. If you don't discipline your children, you are not obeying God.

> *Do not withhold discipline from a child.*
> PROVERBS 23:13 NIV

> *Discipline your children, for in that there is hope.*
> PROVERBS 19:18 NIV

God commands us to discipline our children. Discipline is not an optional part of parenting. It is a matter of obedience to God.

As our Creator, God is the ultimate expert on how to raise children to become wise. He created parents and families for that purpose. He knows what works and what doesn't. If we are wise, we will do what He says.

5. If you fail to discipline your children, you will regret it.

A rod and a reprimand impart wisdom, but a child left undisciplined disgraces its mother. . . . Discipline your children, and they will give you peace; they will bring you the delights you desire.

PROVERBS 29:15, 17 NIV

These two verses paint quite a contrast. On the one hand, an undisciplined child disgraces his mother. But a disciplined child brings delight to his parents. Discipline can make the difference between disgrace and delight.

Proverbs describes two types of parents: the satisfied and the sorrowful. The determining factor is the wisdom or folly of their children. If we want to increase the odds of becoming satisfied parents, we must discipline our children.

Nine Suggestions for Using Discipline Effectively

I considered calling this section "The Nine Commandments of Discipline," but I decided to leave the commanding to God. Nevertheless, Cathy and I found these commonsense suggestions very helpful in using the tool of discipline.

1. *Thou shalt use a combo.* Discipline works best when combined with the other tools of discussion, personal involvement, encouragement, teaching, and prayer. Remember, training is a multifaceted responsibility—stimulating the positive and correcting the negative. If all your parenting is discipline oriented, it will not be satisfying for you or your children. They will develop resentment toward you, and your effectiveness will decrease radically.

2. *Thou shalt be appropriate.* Match the punishment with the crime. Differentiate between immaturity and disobedience, or social missteps and moral wrongs.

A two-year-old who laughs too loudly in a grocery store is being immature. He or she needs parental instruction and time to grow up—not discipline. On the other hand, a child who refuses to come when called is being disobedient and needs discipline.

A four-year-old who belches at the dinner table has committed a social wrong and must be reminded of good manners and warned. Lying, on the other hand, is a moral wrong and must be disciplined.

Reward appropriate behavior and discipline inappropriate behavior. Do not confuse the two. Telling a child you will give him a piece of candy if he doesn't hit his sister is a misuse of a reward and will not build character. Threatening to spank a child if he or she does not get an A on a spelling test is a misuse of discipline. Rewards and discipline are effective when they involve what the child has done, not what he or she *might* do.

3. *Thou shalt remember the goal.* The purpose of discipline is to develop wisdom, not to blow off steam, bolster your ego, or "get back at the little brat." Keeping the goal in mind will guide and enhance the effectiveness of your discipline.

4. *Thou shalt be consistent.* Consistency is more effective than severity. Being firm one day and lenient the next sends a mixed message to the child. Children will test you to see which version they have to deal with that day. They should not have to wonder. As much as possible, they should have loving, warm, firm, clear, stable, positive, wise discipline and encouragement every day.

5. *Thou shalt confirm love.* Children need a strong, consistent confirmation of your love during and after discipline. Remind them of your love when you measure out discipline *and* after it is over. Hold them, hug them, wipe away their tears, and remind them that you love them enough to discipline them.

As a young parent, I was understandably uneasy about spanking my little boys. After spanking them with a little paddle, I held them and expressed my love for them. I always asked, "Do you know that Dad loves you?" Without exception they would say, "Yes, Dad." Notice that I did not ask them if they loved me. I tried that once, and my son looked up and said, "No. From now on, I only love Mommy."

Fortunately, his being upset with me did not last long. By the way, it is best if the one who does the disciplining also does the consoling afterward. Otherwise, the child may not understand the connection between discipline, love, and developing character, and a spirit of division and resentment may be created.

6. *Thou shalt KISS.* The acronym KISS, of course, stands for *Keep It Simple, Stupid.* Discipline works best with a few clearly understood and easily enforceable rules. Focus your rules on the wisdom areas of life, which can be summarized in three words: *respect* (for God, parents, and others), *responsibility* (doing your part without excuses), and *obedience* (do as you're told—immediately, completely, and with the right attitude).

7. *Thou shalt not manipulate or be manipulated.* Parents and children use various means of manipulation, but these strategies undermine and hinder the process of training children to become wise adults.

One common manipulative tool is what we might call *going ballistic.*

Fools give full vent to their rage,
but the wise bring calm in the end.
PROVERBS 29:11 NIV

Discipline is most effective when parents keep their emotions stable. Don't short-circuit effective discipline with foolish behavior. Discipline is best served cool, calm, and collected.

On the other hand, don't allow your children to use anger or tantrums to control you. After they have been rebuked or spanked, do not allow them to pitch a fit. At our house, such behavior merited further discipline.

A second manipulative tool is *guilt-tripping*. Parents can easily use guilt to manipulate their children. They will sigh dramatically and say, "Oh, I'm not angry; I'm just hurt," or, "Do you realize you made Jesus cry?"

As a pastor, I learned long ago that there is only one Holy Spirit, and I'm not Him. It's not my job to make my kids feel guilty. It's the Holy Spirit's job to convict them of their sin. When we try to guilt-trip our kids, it builds resentment and doesn't produce true repentance.

It's important to teach children that their sin does hurt God, and they should confess it to Him. But this need not be a big production and should not include guilt-tripping.

One of the most destructive tools of manipulation that parents and children can use on one another is *conditional love*. Never put conditions on your love. Saying things like, "If you do that again, Mommy will not love you" or "Daddy doesn't love you when you do that," undermines an important foundation of security in your children's lives. It may seem to work at the moment, but it will definitely backfire in the long run.

Children thrive when they are certain of unconditional love from their parents. Even if we don't always love their behavior, we must assure them that we will always love them. After all, God loved us while we were yet sinners (Romans 5:8). He loved us before He cleansed us (Revelation 1:5).

Don't allow a child's threat of withdrawing love to affect you in the least. Kids may say, "If you spank me, I won't love you anymore." Just smile and say, "That is your choice, but I'm still going to love you, and because of your wrong behavior, I'm still going to spank you." Once they realize that you will not be manipulated, they will stop trying to play on your heartstrings.

8. *Thou shalt not be historical.* A fourteen-year-old girl went to her pastor for advice. "What's the problem?" the pastor asked.

"It's my mom," the girl responded. "She is absolutely historical."

"You mean *hysterical*," the pastor replied.

"No, I mean *historical*," the girl insisted. "She never lets me forget anything I've ever done wrong."

Once inappropriate behavior has been disciplined, it should be forgiven and forgotten. When our heavenly Father forgives us, He treats us as if the sin never occurred. The relationship is not affected. The sin is blotted out, hidden behind His back, and cast in the deepest ocean. We will face the consequences of our sins, but God won't use our past sins to shame us. If this is how God treats His children, then we should treat our children the same way.

9. *Thou shalt not be abusive.* Discipline is not and never should be abusive. Physical discipline must always be measured and controlled. It has become popular in some circles to view spanking as primitive and abusive. Critics call it "hitting" and accuse those who practice it of being child abusers. They want to outlaw spanking, as in some Scandinavian countries, for example. Let's take a moment and examine the issue of spanking.

Properly spanking a child is not child abuse. Several commonsense observations need to be made about spanking and child abuse.

a. God tells us to spank (Proverbs 19:18; 22:15; 23:13–14; 29:15). He is not going to tell us to do something abusive.

b. God made children with extra padding on the part of the body that receives the spanking. There are no organs or appendages to be damaged in any way.

c. The goal of spanking is to sting, not to wound.

d. Just because a small minority may misuse spanking does not mean that all who spank are abusive. Those who actually abuse their children should be penalized, not everyone who spanks their kids.

e. Critics of spanking say it promotes violence. In reality, the opposite is true. Since spanking has been outlawed in public schools, violence has increased dramatically. Our local high school recently hired security guards to control violence among the students. When spanking was permissible, this was not necessary.

f. Ultimately, failing to spank is abusive. Proper spanking is not. Failing to spank allows the root of folly to grow to maturity (Proverbs 29:15). Nothing is as dangerous to a child as full-grown folly. God says that failing to spank is a sign of hating your kids (Proverbs 13:24).

g. Spanking should only be one of several disciplinary tools used by parents. Restricting privileges, assigning timeouts, giving verbal rebukes, and grounding are also available means of discipline.

h. Spanking is most effective when it is reserved for major offenses and outright disobedience.

i. Spanking should be done privately and appropriately.

j. Spanking is an effective means of establishing boundaries for young children who test the limits repeatedly to find out who is really in control. The more they are properly spanked before the age of five, the less they will need to be spanked after the age of five.

In raising three very energetic boys, Cathy and I found that we did most of our spanking when they were in the preschool phase of development. Once they discovered we meant business, the need to spank became less frequent. Also, as they got older, alternate forms of discipline became more effective. Still, there were some days when it seemed as if all we did was spank them, especially with our stronger-willed boys. It was not easy, but it was worth it. If you don't win the battle of the wills with a two-year-old, what will you do when he is sixteen and taller than you? Children feel securer with firmly established and enforced boundaries. Discipline, including spanking, is an important part of teaching our kids to walk in wisdom. We fail them if we fail to discipline them.

A Look in the Mirror

Are you willing to properly discipline your children? Are you following the nine suggestions for using discipline effectively? Which one(s) do you need to work on?

Note

1. Dr. Albert Siegel in the *Stanford Observer*, October 1973, 4.

Communicate

"U ncle Bill" Orr has conducted children's crusades throughout the United States and Canada. His accordion, story-telling ability, and warm, twinkling eyes make him an instant hit with kids.

During his crusades he asks his young listeners to complete the sentence, "If I could change anything about my Mom and Dad, I would_____." The responses he receives portray the deep longing children have for better communication with their parents.

"I wish Dad would talk to me."

"I pray my parents would spend more time with me and listen more."

"My mother talks to me, but it's not like the good, close talking I really want. My father doesn't talk to me at all, and I'd like a closer relationship with him."

A recent study of parents of teenagers paints an alarming picture of how little communication actually goes on between parents and teens. Out of 168 hours in a week, the average American teenager spends twenty-six minutes a week talking with his or her dad and fifty-four minutes a week in meaningful conversation with his or her mom. No wonder kids are crying out to their parents, "Talk to me."

When my boys were growing up, I found I needed to plan special times to communicate with each one individually. It may have been a one-on-one breakfast or the drive to or from sports practice, but the boys looked forward to those times when they could talk to me without their brothers around.

Communicate

The rod and reproof give wisdom.
PROVERBS 29:15

The word *reproof* means "to discipline with words." Words impart wisdom, and effective parents know the value of using words to raise wise children. Parenting is such a difficult task that wise parents will use every tool at their disposal. One of our most effective tools is communication.

According to Proverbs, effective parenting is the result of well-communicated lessons and values.

Secret #7 to better parenting:
*Use words to impart wisdom
to your children.*

What Is Impartation?

Impartation means the communication of knowledge. The goal of impartation is for parents to transfer wisdom to their children. Communication that produces wise children involves three major elements: *inclusion*, *reception*, and *motivation*.

Inclusion

Effective parental communication should include every area of life our children will face, presented from God's perspective. For starters, the list would include anger, alcohol, authority, communication, conceit, creation, dating, death, decision-making, faith, fear, friends, God, government, honesty, jealousy, laziness, leadership, life, love, marriage, money, pride, priorities, power, poverty, prosperity, relationships, righteousness, self-discipline, sex, sin, values, women's roles, words, work, and worship.

There should be no major area of life that parents have not discussed biblically and practically with their children. Remember, the goal of parenting is to prepare our children to walk in wisdom in *every* part of life. The challenge is to identify the important areas, know what the Bible says about them, and know how best to share that information with our children.

One night my then-five-year-old son asked me, "Where

do babies come from?" I wanted to say, "Ask your mother," but he obviously wanted to hear it from me. I was glad that I was prepared to begin what became an ongoing discussion about human sexuality, temptation, and marriage that has lasted to this day. The door that was opened at age five has been kept open into adulthood.

By *inclusion*, I mean we should prepare our children to see and respond to every area of life from God's perspective. By the time your children are grown, there should be no closed doors. What I explained to my boys about sex when they were five has needed to be amplified, refined, and further explained as they have gone through adolescence and moved toward marriage.

One of the biggest complaints that teens have about their parents is that when they try to discuss certain subjects (such as sex), the parents "freak out." Effective parents don't freak out. They know that when the door of communication is closed, it is difficult to reopen. So they work to keep the doors of communication open through ongoing discussions of any and every aspect of life.

Think about it. If you don't teach your kids about sex, who will? If you don't teach your children biblical values, who will?

Reception

Impartation assumes that information is not only given but also received. When I ran track in high school, the coach emphasized the importance of passing the baton effectively on relays. We practiced repeatedly until we were able to pass the baton seamlessly while running at top speed. In the process, I learned several lessons:

- Races will not be won unless the baton is passed successfully.
- Passing the baton requires concentration and verbal communication.
- Both the passer and the receiver must participate to pass the baton.

Parenting, at times, is a lot like a relay race. Parents must pass the baton of wisdom to their children. If they fail, the parenting process will not be successful. Also, the successful imparting of wisdom requires concentration and verbal communication; and the parents and children must work together if wisdom is to be imparted from one to the other.

Furthermore, parents cannot impart what they don't possess. If I don't have the baton, I can't pass it to the next runner. Likewise, if I don't possess wisdom, I cannot hope to pass it on to my children. Parents must prepare themselves to pass along wisdom to their kids.

Motivation

Effective parental communication stimulates children in the direction of wisdom. Motivating communication has seven characteristics. It is *purposeful, positive, personal, practical, passionate, plain,* and *potential-focused.*

1. *Purposeful communication* is not just talking to make noise. It is using words to influence your children's lives. It has a goal. It stimulates your children to evaluate life from God's perspective and to make wise decisions.

2. *Positive communication* is *en*couraging, not *dis*couraging. As parents, we must work at selecting positive words and positive tones. Our communication should present the way of wisdom in the most positive light possible.

3. *Personal communication* is tailored to fit a child's age and interests. For example, when my eldest son was eight, he loved sports. To motivate him to pursue wisdom, I spoke to him about star athletes who walk with God. We also discussed athletes who displayed wise character qualities, such as sportsmanship and perseverance, and who overcame obstacles and sacrificed for the sake of their team. Beyond that, we discussed athletes who had fallen because of drug or alcohol abuse or gambling. For him, this approach was very motivating, because he loved sports. Find your

child's hot button and learn to push it.

4. *Practical communication* tells not only *why* but also *how*. It is one thing to tell a child to read the Bible. But it is much more motivating to show a child how to study it. This is true for sharing your faith, praying, resolving conflicts, making decisions, exercising self-control, and making friends. Show them how.

5. *Passionate communication* is based on the principle that values are more often *caught* than *taught*. Before your children will begin to pursue wisdom, they must see that you are passionate about it yourself. To paraphrase Charles Spurgeon, "If you want your children to be hot for God, you must first set yourself on fire." Enthusiasm is motivating.

Passionate parents motivate through the depth of their conviction and the fire of their enthusiasm. But be certain the things that excite you are the things you want to pass on—a love for God's Word, the way of wisdom, and a life of righteousness.

6. *Plain and simple communication* speaks at a level your kids can understand. There is great persuasive power and dignity in simple, straightforward speech. The Lord's Prayer, the twenty-third Psalm, and the Gettysburg Address are examples of concise yet powerful words. Keep it simple, direct, and understandable, and your children will grasp the truth.

7. *Potential-focused communication* motivates by what *can be*,

rather than by what is. We talk to our boys about being "excellers" and not just "existers." The world is full of people who merely exist. They go through life without making much of a contribution to the betterment of the world. God calls us to be people who excel and go beyond the norm. God wants us to make a positive difference in this world.

Seven Methods of Communication

The book of Proverbs employs a variety of communication techniques. When parents get in the habit of using just one method to communicate, their efforts are less effective. Effective parents use a variety of methods to impart wisdom to their children.

As you review the seven methods of communication used in Proverbs, take note of which ones you tend to overuse and those you don't use often enough.

1. *Stories that teach a lesson.* Everyone loves a well-told story. Stories are captivating, illuminating, and easy to remember. Stories told in Proverbs include the following examples:

- the story of rejecting wisdom (1:20–33)
- the story of the ant and the lazy man (6:6–11)

- the story of the young man and the adulteress (7:1–27)
- the story of the call of wisdom (8:1–36)
- the story of the two lifestyles (9:1–18)

When our sons were little, they always asked us to read them a story at bedtime. After Cathy read them a long story—she alternated classics such as *Robinson Crusoe* with contemporary Christian fiction for kids and biographies of Christian heroes—they would often ask, "Now, can you *tell* me a story?"

Cathy invented a series of stories about three little frogs. In an amazing stroke of coincidence, the frogs experienced many of the same events my sons had experienced. Cathy skillfully used these tales to teach timeless truths.

My sons often asked me to tell stories of when I was their age. I enjoyed telling of my many exploits and successes, but they liked it best when I included things I did wrong. No one likes to be compared with a mythical hero. Our kids feel closer to us when we share our struggles and defeats, because we seem more real. I learned to focus my stories of childhood and adolescence on my relationships with God and my parents.

Of course the Bible, especially the Old Testament, contains some of the greatest stories ever told. Moses and Pharaoh, Samson and Delilah, David and Goliath, Daniel in the lions' den, and the prodigal son are just a few timeless classics that children especially enjoy. Occasionally, in the winter months, we acted out stories from the Bible on Saturday evenings. The boys loved to pretend they were Daniel or David. They also enjoyed watching their parents apply their thespian skills with enthusiasm.

Today our sons' favorite Christmas presents are gift cards from the bookstore. They are readers today because they were read to so often when they were little.

2. *Words of motivation and encouragement.* Proverbs often uses positive words of motivation to inspire children to pursue wisdom (3:11–26; 4:1–13), challenging them in the areas of character development and mate selection. It describes the virtues of a good and godly woman (31:10–31) and the importance of marital fidelity (5:15–20), hard work (6:6–8), and righteousness (11:3–6, 8–11). From chapter 10 through 31, approximately one-third of the verses contain at least some word of motivation and encouragement. The themes of wisdom, humility, righteousness, self-control, and fear of God are mentioned often. Wisdom and encouragement go hand in hand.

3. *Rebuke.* Parents must rebuke or correct their children when they get off the path of wisdom.

> *A wise son heeds his father's instruction,*
> *but a mocker does not respond to rebukes.*
> PROVERBS 13:1 NIV

Do not rebuke mockers or they will hate you; rebuke the wise and they will love you. Instruct the wise and they will be wiser still; teach the righteous and they will add to their learning.

PROVERBS 9:8–9 NIV

Effective rebukes will typically include the following steps:

- Get the facts.
- Remain self-controlled.
- Be precise about the offense.
- Let the child explain his or her side of the story.
- Judge actions, not motives.
- Respect the person, rebuke the behavior.
- Make consequences clear.
- Forgive, forget, and move on.

4. *Rules.* Wisdom is a product of discipline. Discipline builds on a few clearly understood and enforceable rules. In our home the rules centered on wisdom gleaned from Proverbs:

- Do not be disrespectful to God or parents.

- Do not lie, cheat, or steal.

- Do not hurt your siblings.

- Do not directly disobey.

5. *Warnings and Challenges.* Though giving wise warnings seems to have fallen out of vogue in our society, they are an essential part of parenting. If we do not warn our kids of certain dangers, who will?

It is difficult for children to consider the results of their behavior. They simply lack the necessary life experience. It is up to their parents to warn them and instruct them.

Everything has an aftermath—and Proverbs is full of such reminders. Our children need to learn that we cannot always judge a decision or an action by its initial stages. Proverbs consistently warns of the negative consequences of poor decisions:

- The aftermath of adultery is bitter and harmful (5:3–5).

- The aftermath of self-centered pursuits is death (14:12; 16:25; 21:6).

- The aftermath of dishonest gain is loss and dissatisfaction (13:11; 20:17).

- The aftermath of evil is bondage (5:22–23).

- The aftermath of folly is ruin (19:3).

- The aftermath of laziness is frustration (15:19).

Proverbs also challenges parents and children with the rewards of good decisions:

- The reward of integrity is security (10:9; 13:6; 28:18).

- The reward of righteousness is eternal life (12:28).

- The reward of honoring God is prosperity (3:9–10).

6. *Personified maxims.* One of my favorite aspects of Proverbs is how it personifies truth with various maxims. We're given brief, clear snapshots of interesting people whose lives illustrate important precepts. Note, for example, Proverbs 10:23 (NIV): "A fool finds pleasure in evil conduct, but a man of understanding delights in wisdom." Both the "fool" and the "man of understanding" are described in one sentence. It is memorable and challenging.

Other personified maxims in Proverbs include the scoffer, the simple, the sluggard, the wicked, the angry, and the hard-hearted. And on the positive side, the wise, the godly, the diligent, the friend, and the righteous.

7. *Value Statements.* It has been said that children in America know the price of everything and the value of nothing. That is a reflection on parents. God has designated us to be the primary value-instillers in our children. We need to teach them what is really important and worth pursuing, sacrificing for, and working toward. We must show them what can bring deep satisfaction and what cannot.

Values are transferred through our example, our attitudes, and our words. In Proverbs, values are often described in short, memorable comparisons. For example, "A good name is more desirable than great riches" (Proverbs 22:1 NIV). A survey of Proverbs reveals at least ten values that parents must communicate to their children.

1. the fear of the Lord (15:16)
2. love (15:17)
3. family harmony (17:1; 21:9, 19)
4. humility (16:19; 25:6–7)
5. honesty (19:22)
6. blamelessness (28:6)
7. self-control (16:32)
8. openness (27:5)

9. loyalty and friendship (27:10)
10. wisdom (16:16)

Earley Family Values

Several years ago, Cathy and I realized that we needed to identify our family's core values. We came up with seven that we wanted to make sure we communicated to our boys.

1. God first
2. family focused
3. church centered
4. love based
5. growth oriented
6. ministry minded
7. excellence oriented

Clearly defining and communicating these values greatly helped us point our children toward wisdom. For example, we encouraged them to spend time with the Lord each day apart from family devotions because our family puts God first. When they got older and had jobs, sports, and ministries, we encouraged them to eat at least one meal at home each day with the rest of the family because we are family focused. They were expected to read and exercise daily because we are growth oriented.

Our family values became an important parenting tool when our eldest son, Daniel, was in middle school. As an elite wrestler, he practiced during the off season with one of the leading clubs in the area. Their tournaments were always on Sunday. Because we were a God-first family and church centered, it was important that Daniel not miss church on Sundays. So he practiced with the team but didn't wrestle in the tournaments.

It wasn't easy for him to go to wrestling practice on Monday night and hear his friends talking about the previous day's tournament, but he did it, and the Lord blessed his commitment. During his eighth grade school season, he went undefeated and unscored upon. In high school he became a state champ and all-American. Most of the boys he wrestled with in that elite club burnt out on wrestling before they reached their potential. Most important, Daniel continues to put God first and is church centered.

A Look in the Mirror

1. How much time have you spent communicating with your children this week? How can you increase your communication?

2. What areas of life have you discussed with your children recently? Which areas are you avoiding? What is your plan for teaching them wisdom?

3. Which of the seven characteristics of motivating communication (purposeful, positive, personal, practical, passionate, plain, potential-focused) are your strengths? Which ones need more work?

4. What communication method (storytelling, rules, rebuke, encouragement, warnings and challenges, personified maxims, or value comparisons) do you need to use more often with your children?

5. Which values do you feel your children have adopted already? Which ones do you need to reinforce more often?

6. Which communication enhancer can you put to work right away with your children?

8 Pray for Your Children

Never underestimate the challenges of parenting.[1] The journey of raising godly kids in an ungodly world is a relentless roller coaster of incredible heights and crushing depths. Joy and sorrow, laughter and tears, fun and frustration crash like waves on our hearts through the events in the lives of our children. Fulfillment and fatigue, exhilaration and exhaustion are all part of the process. Just when we think we have a handle on it, our children reach another stage of development and the path is again shrouded in fog.

Remember, there are no perfect children, no perfect parents, and no perfect parenting situations. Also, no two parenting situations are identical. That is why we need all the help we can get.

Never underestimate the power of prayer. God, who is supremely intelligent and infinitely powerful, already knows and loves your children more and better than you ever will. As you learn to cooperate with Him in prayer, He will show you that He is able to do exceedingly abundantly more than you can ask or imagine.

Cathy and I love our three sons. We believe with all our hearts that the more we pray for them, the more God works on their behalf. We also believe that the more accurately, biblically, and specifically we can pray for them, the more effectively and directly God works in their hearts through the Word of God and their circumstances. Therefore, we try to pray the Bible for them every day.

Secret #8
Consistently pray the Bible for your children.

Ordinary Parents, Extraordinary Results

The Bible offers several examples of ordinary parents whose prayers produced extraordinary results in the lives of their children. Hannah's sincere, selfless, stubborn, sacrificial prayers for a not-yet-conceived son resulted in the birth and life of the great prophet Samuel (1 Samuel 1–16).

A Canaanite mother's persistent, resilient, faith-filled prayers for her demon-possessed daughter brought about a miraculous healing (Matthew 15:22–28).

A government official's simple, direct, faith-filled prayer for his dead daughter touched the heart of God and brought the girl back to life (Matthew 9:18–28).

I am astounded at the number of godly men and women I know

who, when asked for the secret of their spiritual success, point back to the persistent prayers of their parents. Praying for your children will make a powerful, positive difference in their lives.

Why Pray for Your Children?

When I consider the daunting responsibility of trying to influence my children for God, I am stunned by my own insufficiency. I can't do it. But I know someone who can: almighty God. He can do more in seconds than I can accomplish in years. He can produce bigger, better, and longer-lasting results than I can even imagine.

So the question becomes, how can I somehow influence God to be more influential in the lives of my children? The answer, of course, is prayer.

Prayer is powerful.

Because prayer is active cooperation with God on behalf of your children, and because God is almighty, prayer, in a sense, is omnipotent. Pastor R. A. Torrey made this astounding observation:

> *Prayer is the key that unlocks all the storehouses of God's infinite grace and power. All that God is and all that God*

does is at the disposal of prayer. But we must use the key.
Prayer can do anything God can do, and as God can do
anything, prayer is omnipotent.[2]

Missionary Hudson Taylor discovered, "It is possible to move men, through God, by prayer alone."[3] It is also possible to move *children*, through God, by prayer alone.

Prayer goes with your children when you can't.

God is omnipresent. Therefore, prayer is unlimited by space or time. Prayer invites God to work in our children's lives even when we can't be with them.

We can't be with our children 24/7 for the rest of their lives—nor should we want to. But God can, and will, if we pray.

Praying for your children is one of the best ways to love them.

One of the purest and most powerful ways for parents to express and exercise love for their children is through intercessory prayer. Dick Eastman, president of Every Home for Christ, calls it "love on its knees."[4] Intercessory prayer seeks the best for our children before God's throne and brings their needs to the One who has the answer.

Praying for your children gives you necessary wisdom and insight.

Parenting is learned through on-the-job-training and often involves sailing into uncharted waters. As we pray for wisdom, God often reveals the insight we need. James, in his epistle, gives us an amazing promise: "If any of you lacks wisdom, let him ask God, who gives generously to all without reproach, and it will be given him" (1:5).

Praying for wisdom is a request God likes to answer. Solomon is considered the wisest man who ever lived. When he assumed the spiritual responsibility for the "children of Israel," his response was to pray for wisdom.

Give me now wisdom and knowledge to go out and come in before this people, for who can govern this people of yours, which is so great?

2 CHRONICLES 1:10

No one else can pray for your children like you can.

The genuine love you have for your children, the tenderness you feel for them, and your knowledge of their makeup, needs, and problems qualifies you to plead with God on their behalf with an urgency and earnestness that will not be denied. When Jesus wanted to convince us of the Lord's willingness to hear prayer, He based his argument on the power of parental love:

*If you then, who are evil, know how to give good gifts to
your children, how much more will your Father who is
in heaven give good things to those who ask him!*

MATTHEW 7:11

You are responsible for praying for your children.

The responsibility to pray for your children begins and ends
with you. God tells parents, especially fathers, that they are the
ones accountable for the spiritual development of their kids.

*Fathers, do not exasperate your children; instead,
bring them up in the training and instruction of the Lord.*

EPHESIANS 6:4 NIV

*Moreover, as for me, far be it from me that I
should sin against the Lord by ceasing to pray for you,
and I will instruct you in the good and the right way.*

1 SAMUEL 12:23

Why Pray the Bible for Your Children?

When we pray for our children, our prayers need all of the
power we can muster. No other book has a fraction of the power
of the Bible. Our prayers are thus infused with power when we
pray the Bible for our children.

For the Word that God speaks is alive and full of power [making it active, operative, energizing, and effective]; it is sharper than any two-edged sword, penetrating to the dividing line of the breath of life (soul) and [the immortal] spirit, and of joints and marrow [of the deepest parts of our nature], exposing and sifting and analyzing and judging the very thoughts and purposes of the heart.

HEBREWS 4:12 AMP

Praying Scriptures gives divine power and direction to your prayers.

The Bible is God's Word. When we pray the Scriptures, we pray God's words back to Him. The words of Scripture were given to guide us in all areas of life (Psalm 119:105), and every word was written straight from the heart of the greatest Father in the universe to His children. When we pray the Bible, we link our hearts with God's heart on behalf of our children and bring the power of God's promises into their lives.

Praying the Bible is "transacting business" with God.

Missionary Hudson Taylor left a deep mark for God in China and around the world. He founded the China Inland Mission, which grew to include 205 mission stations, more than 800 missionaries, and 125,000 Chinese Christians. Taylor's son and daughter-in-law, in their biography of Hudson Taylor's life, attributed his success to "the simple, profound secret of drawing for every need upon 'the fathomless wealth of Christ.'"[5]

Taylor learned this type of prayer life from his mother and his sister. He was converted through their persistent, prevailing prayers. On the day Hudson made his commitment to Christ, his sister wrote the following words in her diary:

> From the very commencement of my Christian life, I was led to feel that the promises of the Bible are very real, and that prayer is in sober fact *transacting business with God*, whether on one's own behalf or on behalf of those for whom one seeks His blessing.[6]

"Transacting business" with God became a model for Hudson Taylor's dynamic life of bold faith and prayer. Every need, whether for his family, funds, converts, or workers, came by trusting God and claiming His promises.

How to Pray the Bible for Your Children

Pray wisdom into their lives.

Our goal as Christian parents is to raise wise children. The entirety of Jesus' childhood years is summed up in two verses in the Gospel of Luke. Note the prevailing theme:

The child grew and became strong, filled with wisdom.
And the favor of God was upon him.
LUKE 2:40 (EMPHASIS ADDED)

Jesus increased in wisdom *and in stature*
and in favor with God and man.
LUKE 2:52 (EMPHASIS ADDED)

As Jesus grew and became physically stronger, He also developed in the way of *wisdom*. He increased in favor with God and with others. One great Bible prayer to pray for your children every day is that they would grow physically and in wisdom and in favor with God and others.

Pray for your children like Paul prayed for his.

In one sitting, I read each of Paul's prayers for his spiritual children in four translations. Reading them all together shook me, convicted me, challenged me, and powerfully encouraged me as I prayed for my own children. (Paul's prayers are found in Romans 1:8–10; 15:5–6, 13; Ephesians 1:15–19; 3:14–19; Philippians 1:9–11; Colossians 1:9–12; 1 Thessalonians 1:2–3; 3:11–13; 2 Thessalonians 1:11–12; Philemon 1:4–6.) I was reminded of four aspects of Paul's prayers that we can apply as we pray for our children: *consistency*, *gratitude*, *expectation*, and *spiritual focus*.

1. Consistency

The first thing that jumped out at me as I studied Paul's prayers was his repeated mention of how regularly, consistently, constantly, fervently, and frequently he prayed (Romans 1:9; Ephesians 1:16; Colossians 1:3; 1 Thessalonians 1:2–3; 3:10; 2 Thessalonians 1:11; 2 Timothy 1:3; Philemon 1:4–5). You get the idea that he never missed a day, let alone an opportunity to pray for his spiritual children. Every time they came to mind, he offered a prayer on their behalf.

We tend to pray when there is an emergency or crisis but slack off when the pressure eases. We must learn to pray consistently, even when there is no crisis. If we do, there will likely be fewer crises.

How much time do you actually spend praying for your children? Most parents would probably have to say, "Too little, too rarely, and too late." I strongly encourage you to establish a set time, at least once a day, when you pray Scripture for your children.

2. Gratitude

Paul was not only consistent in his prayers but also constant in his gratitude. Again and again he mentions how thankful he is (Romans 1:8; 1 Corinthians 1:4–7; Ephesians 1:15–16; Philippians 1:3–6; Colossians 1:3–4; 1 Thessalonians 1:2–3; 2:13; 3:9; 2 Thessalonians 1:3; 2 Timothy 1:3–5; Philemon 1:4–5).

Parenting can be the most discouraging task we face. Our children go through stretches when they take three steps forward and two steps back. Paul's spiritual protégés could have worn him out and driven him crazy. But they didn't make him bitter, cynical, or discouraged. Why? He always thanked God for them—even for the Corinthians, who struggled to follow his leadership, continually fought with one another, and got off track easily, quickly, and often.

We should also note that Paul was grateful to God for what He had done in everyone's lives. Paul's base of gratitude was *spiritual*, not physical or material. I am not saying we shouldn't thank God for the physical, material, educational, and vocational blessings He gives our children. But the primary content of our gratitude should be focused on the spiritual work He is doing in their lives.

3. Expectation

Paul was also confident in his expectation. He prayed, believing that God was not finished yet.

May the God of hope fill you with all joy and peace in believing, so that by the power of the Holy Spirit you may abound in hope. I myself am satisfied about you, my brothers, that you yourselves are full of goodness, filled with all knowledge and able to instruct one another.

ROMANS 15:13–14

Notice that Paul based his prayers on the confidence he had in God, whose character pervaded the lives of Paul's spiritual children.

I give thanks to my God always for you because of the grace of God that was given you in Christ Jesus, that in every way you were enriched in him in all speech and all knowledge—even as the testimony about Christ was confirmed among you—so that you are not lacking in any spiritual gift, as you wait for the revealing of our Lord Jesus Christ, who will sustain you to the end, guiltless in the day of our Lord Jesus Christ. God is faithful, by whom you were called into the fellowship of his Son, Jesus Christ our Lord.

1 CORINTHIANS 1:4–9

The Corinthians were Paul's most troublesome group of spiritual children. Yet he was confident that one day even they would end up blameless, because *God is faithful*. We can pray for our children with great expectation because we are praying to a great and faithful God.

Every time you cross my mind, I break out in exclamations of thanks to God. Each exclamation is a trigger to prayer. I find myself praying for you with a glad heart. I am so pleased that you have continued on in this with us, believing and proclaiming God's Message, from the day you heard it right up to the present. There has never been the slightest doubt in my mind that the God who started this great work in you would keep at it and bring it to a flourishing finish on the very day Christ Jesus appears.
PHILIPPIANS 1:3–6 MSG

Paul says that he prayed from a foundation of strong confidence that God would gloriously complete the work He had started. There will be times when our children disappoint us. But, like Paul, we must remember to place our faith in God, who is at work in their lives and will complete that work.

Now to him who is able to do far more abundantly than all that we ask or think, according to the power at work within us, to him be glory in the

church and in Christ Jesus throughout all generations, forever and ever.
Amen.

Too often we aim our prayers too low. Paul prayed expectantly that his spiritual children would not merely make God's team and ride the bench, but that they would hit spiritual home runs and end up in the spiritual hall of faith. God is able and willing to do far more than we can ask or imagine.

4. Spiritual Focus

Paul was also consumed with the spiritual progress of those he had brought to Christ. Note the spiritual focus of each of the following prayers:

- that they would know God and all God had available for them (Ephesians 1:17–19)
- that they would have inner strength and live open to Christ, experiencing the full dimensions of His love (Ephesians 3:14–20)
- that they would learn to live wisely and bear spiritual fruit (Philippians 1:9–11)
- that they would be in step with God's will and work for

Him with glorious and joyful endurance (Colossians 1:9–12)

- that they would overflow with love, strength, and purity (1 Thessalonians 3:11–13)
- that God would make them holy and whole inside and out (1 Thessalonians 5:23–24)
- that they would be fit for what God had called them to be (2 Thessalonians 1:11–12)
- that they would experience spiritual encouragement and empowerment (2 Thessalonians 2:16–17)

If you want several good prayers to pray for your children's spiritual development, pray the prayers Paul prayed. Paul's prayers were consumed with the spiritual state of his spiritual children. Moreover, he prayed for their ongoing spiritual development and progress—that they would be "increasing in the knowledge of God" (Colossians 1:10) and would "increase and abound in love for one another and for all" (1 Thessalonians 3:12).

A Look in the Mirror

1. Do you pray for your children?
2. Do you pray for them daily?

3. Do you pray with gratitude?

4. Do you pray expectantly, believing God will work?

5. Do you focus the content of your prayers on their spiritual development?

Notes

1. This chapter was adapted from Elmer Towns and Dave Earley, *Praying for Your Children* (Shippensburg, PA: Destiny Image, 2010).

2. R. A. Torrey, *The Power of Prayer* (Grand Rapids: Zondervan, 1924), 17; emphasis his.

3. Hudson Taylor, as quoted in J. O. Sanders, *Spiritual Leadership* (Chicago: Moody, 1974), 82.

4. Dick Eastman, *Love on Its Knees* (Grand Rapids: Chosen, 1989), 56.

5. Dr. and Mrs. Howard Taylor, *Hudson Taylor's Spiritual Secret* (Chicago: Moody, 1989), 16.

6. Ibid., 19; emphasis added.

9

Partner in Ministry
with Your Children

When Cathy and I graduated from college, my parents gave us one of the greatest presents we have ever received: a trip to the Holy Land. We spent ten days, with a group from my seminary, walking where Jesus had walked. The trip was eye-opening in many ways. After seeing the land of the Bible with my own eyes, Bible reading changed from a nice black-and-white book to a full-color experience.

One of the images that stuck with me was that of the Dead Sea. It is a bizarre place close to where Sodom and Gomorrah are believed to have been. The Dead Sea is actually a large lake, fed primarily by the Jordan River. It is surrounded by cliffs, is more than 1,200 feet deep, and is saltier than the ocean.

The reason it is called the Dead Sea is because there is almost no organic life in its waters. Imagine a lake with no fish or plants. The reason the Dead Sea has no organic life is simple: it has no outlet. Many rich minerals flow into the Dead Sea from the Jordan River, but nothing flows out. Those minerals stay in the water and smother the life from it.

Many Christians are like the Dead Sea. They take in rich deposits of truth and are very deep, yet they are also mostly dead.

Why? Like the Dead Sea, they have no outlet. They never get involved in ministry.

Christianity is all about life. It is an expression of new life in Jesus Christ. Life abounds when truth and the work of the Holy Spirit flow not only into our lives, but also out of our lives. For Christians, the outlet is ministry and evangelism.

One of the simplest ways to raise wise children is to have them serve with you. It is not enough to fill their heads with good information. They need application in order for the information to lead to transformation and life change.

Serve with Your Children

According to statistics quoted by Jerry Pipes and Victor Lee in the book *Family to Family*, "88 percent of those who grow up in our evangelical churches leave at eighteen and do not come back."[1] In other words, only 12 percent of the kids raised in church will stay in church.

What can you do to ensure that your children will stay on the way of wisdom after they leave high school? Get them involved with you in ministry.

According to another study quoted by Pipes and Lee, "When parents lead their children in sharing their faith and engaging the spiritual harvest, the 88 percent fallout drops to less than 4 percent."[2] Serving together with your children will keep them on your team and God's team.

Secret #9
Partner in ministry with your children.

Evangelistic activity deepens spiritual understanding and appreciation.

Recently, a young lady in our home Bible study group shared about the spiritual condition of her graduating class from a Christian school. Seven years after graduation, she could name only two others from a class of fifteen who were still walking with God and involved in church. Why?

Children who grow up in Christian homes often come to faith in Christ at an early age. Often they are sheltered from non-Christians and aren't involved in evangelism with their families. As a result, they too often take their salvation for granted. They don't apprehend and appreciate the life, power, and spiritual blessings available to them in Christ. Consequently, they end up living weak Christian lives and flee into the world when they get a chance.

If we want our children to continue on the way of wisdom, we must get them involved with us in evangelistic activities early and often in their upbringing.

> *I pray that your partnership with us in the faith*
> *may be effective in deepening your understanding*
> *of every good thing we share for the sake of Christ.*
>
> PHILEMON 1:6 NIV

Missional living was and is the prayer of Jesus.

Hours prior to His crucifixion, Jesus prayed for His spiritual children, the eleven remaining disciples. Read His prayer carefully.

> *"I do not ask that you take them out of the world, but that you keep them*
> *from the evil one. They are not of the world, just as I am not of the world.*
> *Sanctify them in the truth; your word is truth. As you sent me into the*
> *world, so I have sent them into the world. . . . I do not ask for these only,*
> *but also for those who will believe in me through their word."*
>
> JOHN 17:15–18, 20

In this section of His prayer, Jesus makes several important observations:

1. His followers are not to isolate themselves from the world.

2. His followers are to be in the world but not swayed by it.

3. by the truth of God's Word.

4. To stay holy in this world, we must focus on rescuing others whom we have been sent to reach. To be a follower of Christ is to be a "sent" one. We must have a missional mind-set and lifestyle.

5. His prayer was not only for his immediate disciples, but also for all who would follow Him down through the ages.

As parents, by making Christ's priorities our own, we can answer His prayer and keep our children on the way of wisdom.

Ministry keeps your children on your team and God's team.

Several years ago, Brad and Lisa joined with several other families from our church to launch a daughter church on the other side of town. At the time, they made an extremely wise decision by including their children in the church-planting effort.

Every Sunday morning, Brad took seven-year-old Josh along with him as he led the setup crew. Together they worked with a few other men to roll out carts, unload the sound system, put up the stage, assemble the nursery and children's areas, and prep the hospitality and information tables. Then they'd go together to breakfast, where Brad led a short Bible study for the setup guys.

After breakfast, Brad and Josh drove home, cleaned up, and

returned to church with Lisa and twelve-year-old Natalie. Lisa and Natalie worked together in the children's ministry and with the children's choir. Every summer, the family served together as Lisa ran the vacation Bible school ministry. Now, nearly ten years later, both Natalie and Josh are still on their parents' team and God's team.

Reg was determined to keep his son, Ryan, on his team and on God's team as they navigated the difficult teen years. Reg's ministry was that of head usher. He coordinated the other ushers and made sure the offering was properly collected and delivered to the safe. Then he joined his wife, Kim, in time for the message. When Ryan turned twelve, he began to work faithfully alongside Reg every Sunday morning. Week after week, year after year, they served together and sat together with Kim in the front row during the worship service. Partially as a result, Ryan successfully passed through the challenges of adolescence while maintaining a close relationship with his father, the church, and God.

"It's Who We Are."

I have led Bible study groups ever since my junior year in high school. And starting when my children were little, we have held a family small group Bible study several nights a week.

When my boys were in middle school, they wanted to reach their unchurched friends for Christ. As a parent, I was not allowed to teach a Bible study in the public schools; but as students, they were. So they started a before-school group that met every Thursday morning. The boys led the study and did all the inviting, contacting, praying, and teaching. I simply sat in the back, watched, and quietly prayed.

When they were in ninth grade, they went to a very large public school and were not quite as confident leading their friends and older kids in Bible study, so they asked me to do the teaching and to have the group meetings at our house. Again, they and their friends did all the inviting, contacting, and praying for the group. They also led the boys in breakout groups. Cathy prepared the house, fixed the snacks, and worked with the girls. I planned the agenda each week and did most of the teaching.

Soon we had as many as sixty students a week coming to our house for Bible study. Having so many kids in our home each week was often challenging and exhausting, but it made an impact. More than half the kids came from unchurched families, and students were saved every month.

We made a positive difference in the lives of many high school students, but we had an even larger impact on our sons. Giving up Wednesday nights to serve high school students as a family was one of the wisest and most effective things we ever did as parents.

Now that my sons are in college, they have all been asked to lead prayer and Bible study groups. My youngest son, Luke, started college early for his age and is therefore younger than all the other leaders in his hall. Yet they have noted his heart for ministry. When someone asked him how he came to be so good at leading a small group, he said, "I've been doing this with my family all my life. It's who we are."

Ministry means serving—together.

Through His word and His example, Jesus taught His followers that ministry means service.

> *"Whoever would be great among you must be your servant,*
> *and whoever would be first among you must be slave of all.*
> *For even the Son of Man came not to be served but to serve,*
> *and to give his life as a ransom for many."*
>
> MARK 10:43–45

> *Have this mind among yourselves, which is yours in Christ Jesus,*
> *who, though he was in the form of God, did not count equality*
> *with God a thing to be grasped, but made himself nothing,*
> *taking the form of a servant, being born in the likeness of men.*
>
> PHILIPPIANS 2:5–7

If we want our children to be like Jesus, we must teach them to be servants. The easiest way for them to learn ministry is to serve alongside us.

The book of Acts tells the story of Paul, the great missionary church planter. As you read of Paul's travels, notice that *he never went alone.* Wisely, Paul always brought along others to work with him.

Paul began his ministry by serving with Barnabas in Antioch (Acts 11:25–30) and going on a missionary journey with him (Acts 13). Then Paul struck out on his own with Silas (Acts 15:40–41; 16:19–25; 17:4–15; 18:5; 2 Corinthians 1:19; 1 Thessalonians 1:1; 2 Thessalonians 1:1), and they were joined by Timothy (Acts 16:3ff; 1 Timothy 1:1–3; Philippians 2:19) and Luke (Acts 16:10; 20:5–6, 13; Philemon 1:24; Colossians 4:14; 2 Timothy 4:11). Aristarchus, Gaius, and Titus also worked alongside Paul at various times (Acts 19:29; 20:4; 27:2; 2 Corinthians 2:13; 7:6–14; 8:6–23; 12:18; Galatians 2:1, 3; Colossians 4:10; Philemon 1:24).

Paul developed his disciples to the point where he could turn significant responsibilities over to them. He sent Timothy to pastor the church at Ephesus, and Titus was sent to Crete.

Last summer I spoke at a church in New Jersey where my son Daniel had served for two summers as a ministry intern. After I spoke, people came up to me, not to comment on my message, but to tell me how much God had used Daniel in their lives. It was great! I had mentored him in ministry for years, and now my efforts were obviously bearing fruit.

Ministry is more caught than taught.

I began to develop a heart for ministry when my mother took me with her as she visited shut-ins every week. I was probably five or six at the time. We baked cookies, cut flowers from Mom's garden, or purchased extra produce at a fruit farm to take with us. In her quiet, behind-the-scenes way, my mother encouraged many lonely and forgotten people each week.

I have to admit that I did not always enjoy it at the time; I would rather have been playing with my friends. But looking back, I can see that it was extremely good for me. Serving got my eyes off of myself and helped me see the needs of others. I learned that a smile, a few words, and a few minutes of time can brighten someone's entire week.

Minister according to your gifts.

In Romans 12 Paul speaks of the variety of functions needed in a healthy body and a healthy church.

For as in one body we have many members, and the members do not all have the same function, so we, though many, are one body in Christ, and individually members one of another. Having gifts that differ according to the grace given to us, let us use them: if prophecy, in proportion to our faith; if service, in our serving; the one who teaches, in his teaching; the one who exhorts, in his exhortation; the one who contributes, in generosity; the one who leads, with zeal; the one who does acts of mercy, with cheerfulness.

ROMANS 12:4–8

My father was not one to visit shut-ins or nursing homes. He had a different way of ministering to others. His gift was giving. There was nothing he loved more than financially helping someone in need. One year for Christmas we opened our presents to find photographs inside. They were pictures of needy families with big smiles on their faces. Dad told us that he had taken some of the money he would have used to buy us Christmas presents and had given it to some families in town that had no money to buy Christmas presents.

The next year he gave each of us a hundred dollars at Thanksgiving, with specific instructions to find a needy family, a charity, or a good cause, and use the money to help meet the need. Then on Christmas morning we would share how we had used our hundred dollars to minister to others. In his way Dad taught us the joy of giving and serving others. He also taught us much about the real meaning of Christmas.

Use your gifts, and have your children accompany you as you serve the Lord.

A Look in the Mirror

1. Are you actively involved in serving the Lord?

2. What is your weekly place of volunteer service in your local church?

3. Are you teaching your children by having them serve alongside you? If not, what is stopping you?

Notes

1. Jerry Pipes and Victor Lee, *Family to Family* (Nashville: North American Mission Board of the Southern Baptist Convention, 1999), 1.

2. Ibid.

10   Teach God's Word

In the United States alone, more than 20 million new Bibles are sold annually, even though the average American home already has at least four copies. However, despite all the Bibles in America, most Americans actually know very little about God's Word. A recent Gallup survey confirmed that the average American has only a limited knowledge of what the Bible says.

George Gallup, founder of the polling firm behind the survey and a prominent evangelical, was greatly dismayed by the results. He concluded, "Americans revere the Bible, but, by and large, they don't read it. And because they don't read it, they have become a nation of biblical illiterates."

The larger scandal is biblical ignorance among *Christians*. Choose whichever survey you like, and the results among Christians will not be much different than those of the population at large.

What can be done? What can we, as Christian parents, do to ensure that our children will understand and follow the teachings of the Bible?

You Are the Answer

Parents must be the first and foremost educators of their own children, diligently teaching them the Word of God. Parents cannot delegate their responsibility to anyone else—be it the youth pastor, Sunday school teacher, or Christian school teacher. God assigned this nonnegotiable and all-important responsibility to *parents*, and it is important for children to see their parents as teachers and fellow students of God's Word.

After the Lord delivered His children, the Hebrews, from slavery in Egypt by a series of miracles, they spent the next forty years wandering in the wilderness because of their lack of faith and rebellion. After the faithless generation died off, as the Lord was preparing to give their children the Promised Land on the east side of the Jordan River, he told Moses to carefully review the Law before all the people.

Hear, O Israel: The Lord our God, the Lord is one. You shall love the Lord your God with all your heart and with all your soul and with all your might. And these words that I command you today shall be on your heart. You shall teach them diligently to your children, and shall talk of them when you sit in your house, and when you walk by the way, and when you lie down, and when you rise. You shall bind them as a sign

on your hand, and they shall be as frontlets between your eyes. You shall
write them on the doorposts of your house and on your gates.

DEUTERONOMY 6:4–9

These six verses, which were vital to the Hebrews in the days of Moses and Joshua, are also highly significant for us today. Let's unpack the central message of this important command to see what it teaches us about better parenting.

1. *Hear.* Teach your children to hear the Word of God by reading it aloud to them. "Faith comes from hearing, and hearing through the word of Christ" (Romans 10:17).

2. *The Lord our God is one.* In a world cluttered with many gods and many other distractions, the truth of God's exclusivity is an important principle for your children to understand. Many problems would be solved if God's people would simply devote their lives to Him, the one true God.

3. *Love the Lord your God with all your heart and with all your soul and with all your might.* Because God is the only true God, it makes sense to give Him our exclusive, unreserved, and total devotion. Unlike pagan deities, God wants a relationship with His people. Jesus made it clear that the command to love God with everything in our being is the first and greatest command

(Matthew 22:37; Mark 12:30; Luke 10:27).

4. *And these words. . .* Jesus said, "It is written, 'Man shall not live by bread alone, but by every word that comes from the mouth of God'" (Matthew 4:4; quoting Deuteronomy 8:3).

5. *These words. . .shall be on your heart.* God doesn't want His words merely to be carved into a stone tablet or etched onto a scroll. His desire is that truth and wisdom will penetrate into our hearts and become second nature. Our goal as parents is to inscribe God's Word onto the hearts of our children.

6. *Teach them diligently to your children.* Too many parents have either neglected teaching their children the Word of God or delegated the responsibility to the church. But God says that it is the *parents'* responsibility to teach the Word diligently to their children. Of course, parents must first know and live the Word of God themselves, because they cannot impart what they do not possess.

Secret #10 to better parenting:
Teach your children the Word of God.

Help Your Children Memorize Scripture

The command to teach our children diligently comes from a Hebrew word that is also used to describe sharpening arrows or whetting a sword. The idea is that parents are to take God's Word and hone the truth so that it will penetrate the minds and hearts of their children. It means to instill, impress, and impart truth and wisdom. It carries the idea of fixing something firmly in the mind through frequent, forceful repetition.

A sword is never sharpened with a single swipe. No, it must be drawn repeatedly against the whetstone. Likewise, in order to help our children learn the Word of God they must hear it repeated over and over until they have memorized it.

Memorization was a prime learning technique in ancient Israel. Beginning at age five, Jewish children memorized large portions of the Torah (Genesis, Exodus, Leviticus, Numbers, and Deuteronomy). As they grew, the older boys went on to learn key portions of the rest of the Old Testament, and the girls learned the Psalms. Memorization was especially important because most people did not have their own copy of the Scriptures. They also didn't have television, video games, cell phones, or computers to distract them. The focal point of family life was learning and reciting the Scriptures.

The goal, of course, was that the Word of God would eventually become more than words in the children's mouths and would begin to guide and direct every aspect of their lives.

Cathy and I attempted two means of helping our children memorize Scripture. During the school year, they were involved in a club program at church in which they memorized a verse or two each week. They started when they were three and continued through sixth grade. Then, during the summer, we gave them "The Summer Challenge." If they memorized selected verses, they would win a prize, such as a shopping trip to the toy store.

The best way we found to memorize was for each person to have a Bible opened to the selected verse or passage. We went around the room from one family member to the next, repeating the verses phrase by phrase, person by person. Using this method, we *saw* the verses as we read them, we *spoke* them when it was our turn to read, and we *heard* them when others read. You would be amazed at how quickly you can learn Scripture by memorizing it with others.

Imagine how many verses of God's Word you and your children could memorize if your family spent an hour each night memorizing the Bible instead of watching television. If I had it to do over again, I would spend more time memorizing Scripture with my children.

Family Devotions

One tool that many families use to teach their children the Word of God is family devotions. When the boys were younger, we had family devotions four nights a week—Monday, Tuesday, Thursday, and Saturday. On Sunday and Wednesday nights, we were involved in various programs at church, and Friday was family fun night.

Family devotions lasted anywhere from ten minutes to an hour, depending on the age of the children, the amount of homework they had, and how late they got home from sports practice. At the designated time, we gathered in the family room with our Bibles. Our agenda was pretty simple: *read*, *discuss*, and *pray*.

We typically took turns reading the selected passage of Scripture, or we would recite the memory verse together and then separately. Of course, when the children were not yet old enough to read, we read the Bible passage, or a story from a Bible story book, to them.

Often I shared what I had studied for my own devotions that morning. About once a week, I asked everyone to share a verse they had been impressed by in their own personal devotions. We usually picked a key passage from the Bible, a book of the Bible, or a biblical theme and stayed with it for a few weeks.

Next we discussed how the Bible applied to our lives. Usually this involved asking a few very simple questions that prompted everyone to think about the Bible passage in light of our circumstances. For example, if we read a passage about fear, the questions might be something like, "What is one thing you fear about the future, and why?" or "What do you fear in reference to school, and why?"

Lastly, we prayed. Often we began by having everyone tell the Lord a few things they were thankful for. Then we would share something we wanted the others to pray for us. The requests might be, "I need help doing well on my test tomorrow" or "Pray for my baseball game tomorrow night." Then each person would pray for the person on their right. After everyone was prayed for, we might go around again and pray for other people—an aunt, grandparent, neighbor, or friend.

Over the years I learned a few valuable lessons about family devotions. These are things I learned the hard way, and that I wish someone had told me about when we first had children.

1. *Be consistent.* Even if you feel as if you are too busy, too tired, or too distracted to have family devotions, do them anyway. They don't have to be long, but the power of family devotions comes from a consistent commitment to God and His Word. When it's

not going well or everyone is distracted or tired, shorten the Bible time, pray, and call it good. When your children become adults, they will value your consistency.

2. *Press on.* When your kids are little, they may not sit still for very long or stay focused easily. But don't throw up your hands and quit in disgust. Press on anyway. Children often absorb more than you realize. Plus, having regular devotions underscores the priority you give to God.

3. *Don't take yourself too seriously.* Sometimes little kids, or teenagers for that matter, are just plain squirrelly, giggly, wiggly, and rambunctious. Stay even-keeled and positive. Stay focused, and keep it moving. Call on the wiggly one to read, answer a question, or pray. Laugh at your little ones and with them when it's appropriate.

4. *Be personally excited about the Bible and prayer.* The attitude you bring to devotions will be the attitude your children will adopt. Let them see in your face and hear in your voice that you believe God's Word is important and that prayer is a delight.

5. *Be open and honest.* When you pray or answer questions, be honest. As your children get older, they will see through any pretense and see it as hypocrisy. If you are struggling with something, admit it (within the bounds of propriety). Your

children will be as open and honest with you and with God as they see you being.

Apply the Word of God in Everyday Situations

One way we applied the Bible was to pray every time we got in the car. No matter where we were going or who was in the car with us, we prayed about the safety of the trip and the events that were to follow. This was especially interesting when I picked up my boys and some of their friends from ball practice. We did not force their friends to pray, but after a few times they would usually try it, offering a halting sentence or two of thanks for the practice or help with the next game, or asking for safety on the way home. Many young men in our community prayed out loud for the first time in their lives as we gave them a ride home from practice. Many ended up visiting our church for vacation Bible school or later came to our home for Bible study when they were in high school. This habit of prayer also positioned my boys as missionaries to their friends. Many of their friends ended up giving their lives to Christ.

A Look in the Mirror

Here are a few suggestions to help you get started with a personal study of God's Word.

1. *Have a set time.* Whether it's first thing in the morning, last thing at night, or on a break at work, it doesn't matter. What matters is that you pick a time.

2. *Determine an amount of time.* You may start with five minutes, or you may spend an hour. What matters is making it consistent.

3. *Find a place.* It may be at the kitchen table or at your desk—wherever you're most comfortable. (One of my places is in the car; I listen to the Bible on CD in my car every morning.) What matters is that you have a place.

4. *Have a plan.* Maybe you will read one chapter of the Bible a day. For example, Proverbs has thirty-one chapters, corresponding to the number of days in a month. Or you could read through the Bible in a year by reading three chapters a day. Or you could read through the book of Psalms in a month by reading five chapters a day. What matters is having a plan.

5. *Let God speak to you.* Don't just read the Bible so you can check it off on a chart. Read it to meet God and hear what He has to say to you that day.

Once you have established your personal devotions, you can apply the same five steps to establish a time of family devotions with your children. There are many excellent resources available at your local Christian bookstore to help you devise an age-appropriate plan.

Encourage Your Children

*E*ncourage *me.*" Maybe your children aren't old enough to talk, or maybe they simply haven't said those words out loud in recent days. But chances are they have shaped those words in the silent hallways of their souls countless times. Everyone craves encouragement, but especially our children. They are looking for it, longing for it, and listening for it—and the one they seek it most from is you.

Two thousand years ago, the apostle Paul wrote a letter to the church at Colosse, giving them many powerful truths and practical insights. Near the end of the letter, he turned his focus to the family and provided powerful commands to both children and their parents.

> *Children, obey your parents in everything, for this pleases the Lord.*
> *Fathers, do not embitter your children, or they will become discouraged.*
> COLOSSIANS 3:20–21 NIV

Let's unpack this important verse.

Children. This term describes any offspring still under parental control, regardless of age.

Obey your parents in everything. The word used for "obedience" encompasses both actions and attitudes. It speaks of a voluntary submission to authority. This obedience is not to be selective.

For this pleases the Lord. When children obey their parents in this way, such obedience pleases the Lord. Elsewhere in Scripture, children are told to honor their parents (Exodus 20:12) and to listen to their parents' instruction and obey it (Proverbs 1:8; 6:20). Disobedience to parents is a mark of ungodliness (2 Timothy 3:2; Romans 1:30). Disrespect is not to be tolerated (Proverbs 30:17). God takes obedience so seriously that He said that striking or cursing a parent was punishable by death (Exodus 21:15–17; Leviticus 20:9; Matthew 15:4–5; Mark 7:10–13), as was continual disobedience (Deuteronomy 28:18–21).

Because God places parents in the lives of children to provide protection, direction, and character development, obedience helps children realize their potential and enjoy long life (Ephesians 6:3).

Fathers. Though many Bible versions translate the word *pateres* as "fathers," it is actually a more general term meaning *parents.* Paul is speaking to mothers as well as fathers.

Do not embitter your children. Because children are to obey their parents in everything, parents have a tremendous responsibility not to misuse their legitimate authority. The command not to embitter is in a verb tense that emphasizes continual action. Of course we will frustrate our children on occasion, but we must be careful not to continually stir up, provoke, irritate, or exasperate them.

Or they will become discouraged. The word *discouraged* means "to be without courage." It implies losing heart, being listless, spiritless, disinterested, moody, sullen, or having a blank resignation toward life. The role of parenting is to *en*courage, or put godly courage into the hearts of our children. Our culture is focused on building self-confidence, but that is not a biblical perspective. Scripture indicates that we should do our best to root out our children's *self*-confidence and build in a confidence in God.

In Ephesians Paul gives a comparable command to parents:

> *Fathers, do not exasperate your children; instead,*
> *bring them up in the training and instruction of the Lord.*
> Ephesians 6:4 niv

Fathers, do not exasperate your children. Again, the verb denotes continuous action—"do not continually or repeatedly provoke your children."

Instead, bring them up in the training. . . The role of parenting is mostly positive. Fathers especially must tenderly nourish their children to maturity. This command addresses many of the activities of child rearing. It speaks of training in proper conduct and correcting improper behavior. It relates to the cultivation of mind and morals. It uses commands and admonitions as well as reproof and punishment. It includes rules, regulations, rewards, and punishments.

Bring them up in. . .[the] instruction of the Lord. Whereas *training* speaks of the *actions* parents use, *instruction* speaks of the *words* parents use. *Instruction* literally means "training by mouth." This includes teaching by praise, warning, censure, or explanation. It involves giving spoken advice, direction, correction, and encouragement.

The training and instruction of the Lord. Paul frames all of his parenting instruction in the phrase "in the Lord." Our parenting must have a spiritual bent. The point is to get our children to conform not to us, but to the Lord. We want to set them on the way of wisdom—God's way.

Combining these two commands, it becomes clear that one of the most obvious, yet often overlooked, secrets of wise parenting is making sure that our efforts are *encouraging* our children in the right direction. Too many times we are guilty of saying or doing things that discourage our children. The goal of good parenting is to rear children who are highly motivated to make the right choices and choose the way of wisdom.

Secret #11 to better parenting:
Encourage your children.

How to Encourage Your Children to Follow You, Fear God, and Walk in Wisdom

1. Set a good example.

A father took his two little boys for a game of miniature golf. The man at the ticket counter said, "It's three dollars for anyone over six." The father replied, "He's three and his brother is seven, so I guess I owe you six dollars."

The man at the counter said, "Hey, mister, you could have saved yourself three bucks. You could have told me the older boy was six, and I never would have known the difference." That's true," the father replied, "but the boys know the difference."

That wise father realized that one of the best gifts he could give his sons was an example of integrity. Children become embittered and exasperated when their parents fail to live with integrity.

As parents, we must understand that our example will either encourage our children toward wisdom or discourage them. Children are most motivated to move toward God when they see it consistently modeled by their parents.

2. Give them unconditional love.

Nothing encourages a child more than unconditional love. A friend once observed that parents should treat their children as if they have a sign on their forehead that reads, "Love me!" In many ways, through their words and actions, children are continually asking their parents, "Do you love me?"

Children become confused and insecure when they fail to sense unconditional love. The presence of unconditional love almost always improves behavior, but conditional love ultimately produces poor behavior.

God the Father loves us with a powerful, undeniable, unrelenting, unconditional love (Romans 5:8). His loving-kindness is what draws us to repentance (Romans 2:4). We need to pass that love on to our children.

Paul captures the essence of unconditional love in his first letter to the Corinthians. Read the list slowly through the lens of your love for your children.

Love never gives up.
Love cares more for others than for self.
Love doesn't want what it doesn't have.
Love doesn't strut,
Doesn't have a swelled head,

> *Doesn't force itself on others,*
> *Isn't always "me first,"*
> *Doesn't fly off the handle,*
> *Doesn't keep score of the sins of others,*
> *Doesn't revel when others grovel,*
> *Takes pleasure in the flowering of truth,*
> *Puts up with anything,*
> *Trusts God always,*
> *Always looks for the best,*
> *Never looks back,*
> *But keeps going to the end.*
> 1 CORINTHIANS 13:4-7 MSG

3. Fill their tanks.

One of the easiest and most effective ways to encourage your children is to keep their emotional tanks full. Children are easily embittered, discouraged, and exasperated when their emotional tanks are empty. The emotional "fuel" that children run on can be summarized with four As: *acceptance, affirmation, affection,* and *attention.*

Acceptance includes unconditional love but also extends to teaching your children that they are special, unique, and wonderful the way God made them. Like me, all of my sons are less than average in height. As they were growing up, however, we consistently taught them that the stature of a man is measured not in feet and inches but in the size and quality of his character. God has given us, as parents, the responsibility of molding our children into men and women of God.

Affection is vital to your children's ability to receive instruction and stay encouraged. Research has shown a clear correlation between discipline problems at school and inadequate physical affection at home. This is especially true of boys, who need appropriate and consistent affection from their fathers.

Children's ability to deal comfortably with their sexual identity corresponds to the physical affection they receive from their father. Children of all ages need regular doses of affectionate words and touches from both parents. Kisses, hugs, pats on the head, and other appropriate displays of love fill a child's emotional tank. Make it a habit to tell your children that you love them at least once a day.

Affirmation is an important *stabilizer* in your children's lives. Young adolescents especially need to be affirmed in who they are. They are already aware of their shortcomings. If your children's hearts are full of positive affirmation, they will have something to draw on when negative things happen in their lives. Take note of your children's good points and positive qualities, and remind them often. Children will gravitate to wherever they feel affirmed and accepted. If you want your children to be drawn to you, you must be a source of affirmation and acceptance.

Attention is the glue that holds the four As together. Gifts, treats, toys, and trips are no substitute for a parent's personal attention. The more attention you give your children apart from discipline, the better the discipline will be received and the less discipline will be needed.

Discipline problems are often a signal that a child needs more positive parental attention. If your children can't get your attention with good behavior, they will often try to get it with bad behavior. Children with full emotional tanks desire to please their parents. They do not want to disobey.

4. Love your mate.

Loving your mate is one of the best things you can do for your children. Children desperately need the security of having parents who love each other and love them. All else being equal, the better the marriage, the easier it is to parent and the easier it is for the children to walk in wisdom. The reverse is also true.

Moreover, one of the best ways you can prepare your children to have a strong marriage is to have one yourself. Give them a good model to follow. In an age when divorce is widespread, I strongly encourage you to work on your marriage and love your mate. If for no other reason, do it for the sake of your children.

> *"A new commandment I give to you, that you love one another:*
> *just as I have loved you, you also are to love one another. By this all people*
> *will know that you are my disciples, if you have love for one another."*
>
> JOHN 13:34–35

The Bible is clear when it states, "Husbands, love your wives" (Ephesians 5:25). Even if your mate does not reciprocate, the Bible insists: "You shall love *your neighbor* as yourself" (Matthew 22:39, emphasis added). Even if your mate opposes you, there is no excuse not to love. The Bible says, "Love *your enemies*, do good to those who hate you, bless those who curse you, and pray for those who spitefully use you" (Luke 6:27–28 NKJV, emphasis added).

5. Admit your mistakes.

You are not perfect. No one is. And believe it or not, your children know that you are not perfect. So when you make a mistake, be honest and admit it.

In our family, we practice what we call the Twelve Golden Words. When spoken with sincerity, they work wonders when it comes to reconciling differences and keeping the channels of communication clear.

The Twelve Golden Words are actually four short but sweet sentences:

"I was wrong."
"I am sorry."
"Please forgive me."
"I love you."

Numerous times, I have had to say to one of my sons, "I was wrong when I ——— (be specific). I am sorry for ———, because I know that it hurt you. Please forgive me. Even when I don't get it right, I always love you."

Admitting mistakes keeps your children from becoming embittered and exasperated. It will not only increase their respect for you, will also give them a model for how to reconcile relationships.

6. Be there.

What children want most from their parents is simply for them to be there. Children become embittered and exasperated when their parents aren't there for them.

Being there doesn't have to be elaborate. More often than not, it is simply paying attention to the little things that add up to make a big difference in a child's life.

Erin Kurt spent sixteen years teaching school and serving as a nanny in countries around the world. Recently she publicized an assignment she gave her students every year at Mother's Day. The assignment was to list things they remembered and loved most about their mothers. Here is her list of the top ten things students around the world said they remembered and loved most about their mothers.

1. Come into my bedroom at night, tuck me in, and sing me a song. Also tell me stories about when you were little.

2. Give me hugs and kisses, and sit and talk with me privately.

3. Spend quality time just with me, not with my brothers and sisters around.

4. Give me nutritious food so I can grow up healthy.

5. At dinner talk about what we could do together on the weekend.

6. At night talk to me about anything: love, school, family, and so on.

7. Let me play outside a lot.

8. Cuddle under a blanket and watch our favorite TV show together.

9. Discipline me. It makes me feel like you care.

10. Leave special messages in my desk or lunch bag.[1]

A Look in the Mirror

1. How can you better encourage your children and motivate them toward God?

2. Do you need to work on improving your example of godly integrity?

3. Do you need to show more unconditional love?

4. Do your children need to see you loving your mate?

5. Are there some mistakes you need to admit?

6. Do you need to work more on being there for your children?

Note

1. Erin Kurt, "The Top 10 Things Children Really Want Their Parents to Do with Them," ErinParenting.com, http://www.erinparenting.com.

12   Offer Your Children to God

One of the most challenging stories in the Bible is the story of God's command to Abraham to sacrifice his beloved son Isaac on an altar at Mount Moriah. This story challenges me both as a Christian and as a parent. Will I put God first? Will I put God above myself? Will I put God above my kids?

Apparently, in Abraham's day, sacrificing a child to the gods was a common practice among the pagans. But no one would expect God to command Abraham to sacrifice Isaac. Isaac was not only Abraham's dearest possession but also the son of the promise. To kill him would kill the promise. That would be asking too much. It was an immense test of Abraham's allegiance. It did not make sense.

When the Lord asked Abraham to sacrifice Isaac, He was asking Abraham to do the hardest thing imaginable. As any parent knows, Abraham would have much rather been told to sacrifice himself than to sacrifice his son.

But the magnitude of the test is not the most amazing part of the story. There is no indication that Abraham argued with or questioned God. He simply got up early the next morning, saddled his donkey, cut wood for the burnt offering, and set off with Isaac and two servants (Genesis 22:3). But even that is not the most amazing part of the story.

> *On the third day Abraham looked up and saw the place in the distance. He said to his servants, "Stay here with the donkey while I and the boy go over there. We will worship and then we will come back to you."*
>
> GENESIS 22:4–5 NIV

Don't miss that last sentence. Hear exactly what Abraham said that he and Isaac would do: "We will worship and then we will come back." Later he would raise his knife to sacrifice his dearly beloved son, but Abraham did not see his action as a sacrifice. He saw it as worship. For Abraham, worship was the ultimate obedience.

For Abraham, to worship meant to make God his highest priority and obedience to God his only alternative. To worship God meant to obey, no matter how high the price or how personal the loss.

It is important to note that this is the first mention of the word *worship* in the Bible. Therefore, it is the foundation on which our understanding of worship throughout the Bible is to be understood.

At the heart of worship is the concept of *worth*—namely, that

God is worth everything, and thus our worship is an expression of our esteem and honor for God. Our worship affirms that God is worth our ultimate obedience

So a logical question would be, why did God do this?

First, the command was *to test Abraham's priorities* (Genesis 22:1). This ultimate act of faith, obedience, and worship would reveal who was really first in Abraham's life—his son or God.

Often I hear people who think they are being good parents say, "Well, you know the kids come first." But that is not a biblical perspective.

In my thirty years of ministry, I have observed two common traps in contrast to right, biblical priorities:

The trap of the poor parent is putting *self* first.
The trap of the good parent is putting the *child* first.
The priority of really good parents are God first, spouse second, child third.

God first is the only way life works. Why? Because whatever we put first is our actual god. And though children are wonderful treasures, they make lousy gods. In fact, everything makes a lousy god except God himself. God is the only One who is infinite, perfect, and true. No one has perfect kids. No one's kids have unlimited power, wisdom, knowledge, love, righteousness, and grace.

If you don't put God first, you will not be the best parent you can be. You will have unrealistic expectations of your kids, because subconsciously you expect them to meet needs in your life that only God can meet. Second, when God asked Abraham to sacrifice Isaac, it may have been to remind Abraham (and us) that children are gifts on loan to us from God. Children are the most precious treasures we have. In fact, the Bible says they are a reward from God (Psalm 127:3). Nevertheless, they really belong to God. He puts them in our families for a time, but they ultimately belong to Him.

A third reason that God asked Abraham to sacrifice his son was to foreshadow the day when *God himself would sacrifice His Son*, in order that all who believe in Him will have eternal life (John 3:16).

Fortunately, Abraham did not have to kill his beloved son. God provided another sacrifice on the mountain (Genesis 22:6–18), just as he would thousands of years later on the mountain of Calvary.

Secret #12 to better parenting:
Offer your children to God.

Give Your Children to God

In our two decades of parenting, Cathy and I have found it very helpful to dedicate our sons to God and to keep reminding ourselves that they are God's children on loan to us.

When Cathy became pregnant with Daniel, our eldest, we were ecstatic. Previously, Cathy had been unable to conceive, and we had prayed and promised God that we would dedicate to Him any children He saw fit to give us.

Six months into the pregnancy, something terrible happened. Cathy went into labor, and we rushed to the emergency room. She nearly lost the baby before the doctors were finally able to stop her contractions. As I drove away from the hospital later that night, I had tears running down my cheeks and a knot in the pit of my stomach. I remembered telling God that if He would give us a boy, we would give him back to God. But when faced with the possibility of losing our son, such an ultimate sacrifice seemed much easier said than done.

I prayed, "Lord, we don't understand why You would give us a baby boy and then take him away. But You are God, and I am not. I will trust You no matter what."

The rest of the story is that after months of bed rest and medication, Cathy delivered a healthy baby. Today Daniel is a highly committed Christian who is studying to become a pastor.

"As for me and my house. . ."

After forty years of wandering in the wilderness, Joshua led the Hebrew nation into the Promised Land. For the next forty years, he led them to become established as a nation in the land.

Shortly before he died, Joshua assembled the people so he could give them some final instructions. In his famous last speech, he challenged the Israelites to continue to follow God. Then he said, "But if serving the LORD seems undesirable to you, then choose for yourselves this day whom you will serve, whether the gods your ancestors served beyond the Euphrates, or the gods of the Amorites, in whose land you are living. But as for me and my household, we will serve the LORD" (Joshua 24:15 NIV). Whom you will serve is your own choice. No one can make it for you. But you can make it for yourself and your family if you will dedicate yourself and your children to serve the Lord and not other gods.

A "god" is anything that takes precedence in time, attention, energy, and direction. In Joshua's day, the false gods were obvious. They were statues and carvings. In our day, the false gods are not as evident but are just as real. Let's be honest. How many people say God is God, but when push comes to shove, their job or career is really their god, or their hobby, material possessions, or money is their god.

It is not enough to dedicate our children to the Lord; we must also dedicate ourselves. If we want God to be first in our children's lives, we must make sure that He is first in our own.

I have found that one measure of the place God holds in my life is how I spend my time and money. Jesus said, "Where your treasure is, there your heart will be also" (Matthew 6:21). If we love God above all else, we will consistently invest in His kingdom and His work.

My father was a generous giver, and he taught me to put God first by giving to His kingdom first. When I was very little, my father gave me an allowance of thirty cents a week. He wisely instructed me to put ten cents in the offering at church and another ten cents into my savings account; then I could do with the remaining ten cents whatever I wished. By this simple act, he taught me the value of giving to God and saving for the future. As a result, I have never struggled to give to God or to save.

If God is first in our lives, we will spend our time—especially our discretionary time—serving Him. We all are given twenty-four hours a day, 168 hours a week, 8,736 hours a year, and 611,520 hours in a lifetime (if we live to be seventy years old). We should consistently invest our time in serving God and advancing His kingdom.

"I will give him to the Lord."

I love the story of Hannah and Samuel. Hannah was a godly woman who desperately desired to have a child but was barren (1 Samuel 1:2). Year after year she prayed, and year after year she remained childless. Finally, she went to God with relentless faith, fasting, and prayer. I believe she had reached the place where she did not want a baby for herself but as a future leader who could turn her nation back to God. So she made a promise:

> *"Lord Almighty, if you will only look on your servant's misery and remember me, and not forget your servant but give her a son, then I will give him to the Lord for all the days of his life."*
>
> 1 SAMUEL 1:11 NIV

God answered her prayer with a precious baby boy, whom she named Samuel (1 Samuel 1:19–20). The name Samuel literally means "God heard." Hannah was obviously delighted that God had heard her prayer.

When Samuel was old enough, Hannah fulfilled her promise and gave him back to God to serve him with his life. Samuel grew up to be a great man of God, a man who helped lead Israel back to God.

It must have taken strong faith and courage for Hannah to

fulfill her promise and give little Samuel so tangibly to the Lord that she left him in the care of Eli the priest to raise him in the temple. In light of the way Hannah gave her little boy to God, I am troubled when I hear parents worry when their children make decisions to follow God. These parents don't want their teenagers to go on mission trips because they are afraid they might get hurt. They worry about them becoming missionaries because they might be called to live in a hard and dangerous place. Some parents don't want their children to become pastors or to marry pastors because they are afraid they will face financial challenges all their lives. What shortsighted, horizontal thinking.

Let me ask you a very significant question: "How big is God?" The answer: "Big enough!"

God is big enough to take care of your kids. You can rest assured that the infinite, almighty, all wise God is big enough to take care of your children. The safest place on this planet is in the will of God. The most unsafe place on this planet is outside of the will of God. Sometimes I fear that overprotective parents "protect" their children right out of God's will for their lives.

Hannah turned little Samuel over to God and to live with Eli at a very young age. He went into a very difficult situation, yet he was right where God wanted him to be. God was big enough not only to take care of Samuel, but more important, to also use him to lead the nation of Israel back to God. Wouldn't it be wonderful if your children grew up to be like Samuel, living right in the middle of God's will and leading their nation back to God?

"To present Him to the Lord"

Forty days after Jesus was born, Mary and Joseph took him to the temple in Jerusalem. They offered a little sacrifice and presented Jesus to the Lord.

> When the time came for their purification according to the Law of Moses, [Joseph and Mary] brought [Jesus] up to Jerusalem to present him to the Lord.
> LUKE 2:22

This passage helps us realize that the act of dedication is in many ways more for the parents than for the child. Jesus, the Son of God, did not *need* a dedication ceremony. He was God. But I believe it was necessary for Mary and Joseph's sake. They needed to remember that this miraculous, virgin-born baby really belonged to God—as do all babies. So they went to the temple and presented Him to God.

When our boys were infants, we participated in a special service of child dedication at our church. It was a meaningful time in which we publicly dedicated ourselves and our babies to the Lord. We pledged to be godly examples and to raise them in the church to love and serve the Lord.

In the process, we identified ourselves with Abraham, saying that we were willing to present the most precious things in our lives to God. We identified with Joshua, declaring that we would serve the Lord and not false gods. Like Hannah, we were willing to give our children back to serve the Lord. And like Mary and Joseph, we presented our treasured babies to the Lord.

Keep on Giving Them to God

Apart from a special church ceremony to dedicate our children to the Lord, how can we continually live out this principle of giving our children back to God? One example is to present our children back to God each day in prayer. Mirroring the attributes of Jesus described in Luke 2:40, we can make it our daily prayer that our children will grow, become strong in spirit, and be filled with wisdom, and that the grace of God will be upon them.

We should also give our children back to the Lord at defining transitional times in their lives. We should remind ourselves that our children have been offered to the Lord when they move into new phases of life, such as the first day of school, when they go on their first mission trip, when they drive for the first time on their own, when they begin their first job, when they start high school, when they leave for college, when they get their own apartment, when they graduate from college, when they get married, and when they have their own children.

A Look in the Mirror

1. Do you need to put God first above all other gods?

2. Do you need to put God ahead of your kids?

3. Have you given your kids up to serve God in whatever way He may direct?

4. Do you need to be more committed to raising your kids for God? Do you need to spend more time in this pursuit?

5. Do you need to make better use of the church to help you raise your kids for God?

6. Do you need to dedicate your kids to the Lord the next time your church has a children's dedication service?

7. Will you give your children back to the Lord daily in prayer?

Teach Your Children to Experience God for Themselves

Did you know that eighty-six of the first colleges established in the United States were designed to promote the claims of Jesus Christ? The list includes Harvard, Yale, and Princeton, which were founded to train pastors. Harvard, the first college in America, adopted the motto "Truth for Christ and the Church" in 1692. Its early rules and precepts included the following provisions:

> Let every Student be plainly instructed, and earnestly pressed to consider well, the main end of his life and studies is to know God and Jesus Christ, which is eternal life (John 17:3); and therefore to lay Christ in the bottom, as the only foundation of all sound knowledge and Learning. And seeing the Lord only giveth wisdom, let every one seriously set himself by prayer in secret to seek it of him (Proverbs 2:3).
>
> Every one shall so exercise himself in reading the Scriptures twice a day, that he shall be ready to give such an account of his proficiency therein, both in Theoretical observations of Language and Logic, and in practical and

spiritual truths, as his Tutor shall require, according to his ability; seeing the entrance of the word giveth light, it giveth understanding to the simple (Psalm 119:130).[1]

With such a strong foundation in Christian life and principles, what happened?

Our public school system was established in 1647 with the Bible as its chief curriculum. Yet last year a teacher was fired from one of our public schools for simply having a Bible on her desk.

What happened?

As many as 88 percent of churched high school students drop out of the church—permanently—by the time they graduate from college.

How could this happen?

Why do godly parents often raise children who grow up with no interest in spiritual things? Nothing would break my heart more than if my sons grew up cold and dead to Christ. As Christian parents, what can we do to prevent that from happening? How can we keep our children from becoming spiritual castaways?

To answer these questions, we must understand the concept of first-, second-, and third-generation spirituality.[2] This principle, which is found throughout the Bible, is seen most clearly at the end of the book of Joshua and in the second chapter of Judges.

The First Generation

At the end of the book of Joshua, when the great leader gives his farewell address and challenges the nation of Israel to "choose this day whom you will serve," we don't often pay close attention to the response of the hearers. Like Joshua, they also make a pledge of loyalty to the Lord, but note carefully that they base their commitment on their *personal experiences* with the Lord:

> *Then the people answered, "Far be it from us that we should forsake the Lord to serve other gods, for it is the Lord our God who brought us and our fathers up from the land of Egypt, out of the house of slavery, and who did those great signs in our sight and preserved us in all the way that we went, and among all the peoples through whom we passed."*
>
> JOSHUA 24:16–17

Notice that they referred to the Lord as "the Lord *our* God." Notice also that they pledged not to forsake Him because He "did those great signs in our sight."

This first generation of Promised Land people were highly committed to God because they had personally seen Him do great things as He delivered them from Egypt and preserved them in the wilderness. As children, they had witnessed the ten plagues and the parting of the Dead Sea. They had tasted with their own mouths the manna from heaven. They had seen the pillar of cloud guiding them by day and the pillar of fire at night. They had crossed into the Promised Land on dry land as they saw God miraculously part the Jordan River. They had marched around Jericho for seven days and had seen God knock down the massive walls of the city. They had a personal commitment to God based on a personal relationship with God because of their personal experience with God.

Not only was this generation the *first* generation to inhabit the Promised Land, but they were also the first generation to experience God's miraculous work in delivering His people from Egypt. First-generation followers of God tend be highly committed to Him because of the wonders He has done in their lives.

The Second Generation

This first generation had children, whose story is concisely recorded in the second chapter of Judges. Read it carefully.

> *And the people served the Lord all the days of Joshua,*
> *and all the days of the elders who outlived Joshua, who had*
> *seen all the great work that the Lord had done for Israel.*
>
> JUDGES 2:7

So this second generation also served the Lord—during the lifetime of their parents; but notice that the verse specifies that it was their parents "who had seen all the great work that the Lord had done for Israel." The second generation maintained a level of spiritual commitment because of their parents' experience and relationship with God. But this generation did not have their own personal experiences. The only miracles they knew of were the ones their parents had told them about. Second-generation followers of God tend to serve the Lord, but usually with less commitment and fervency than their parents because they haven't seen His works in their own lives.

The Third Generation

The second generation also had children. This third generation grew up to become the adult leaders of Israel, but they lacked the personal experience with God that their grandparents had enjoyed. All they had to go on was the tepid spiritual commitment of their parents. Their story is one of the saddest in the Bible:

> *And all that generation also were gathered to their fathers.*
> *And there arose another generation after them who did*
> *not know the Lord or the work that he had done for Israel.*
> JUDGES 2:10

This third generation of Israelites "did not know the Lord." In the language of the Old Testament, "knowing the Lord" is synonymous with personal salvation. Even though their grandparents had been rescued from Egypt by the mighty hand of the Lord, they did not believe in the God of their grandparents.

According to Judges, not only did the third generation not know the Lord, but they also were unfamiliar with the works that God had done to rescue and preserve Israel. They had never personally experienced God's works in their generation. Therefore, they had no commitment to the Lord and quickly turned to worshipping idols.

And the people of Israel did what was evil in the sight of the Lord and served the Baals. And they abandoned the Lord, the God of their fathers, who had brought them out of the land of Egypt. They went after other gods, from among the gods of the peoples who were around them, and bowed down to them. And they provoked the Lord to anger. They abandoned the Lord and served the Baals and the Ashtaroth.

JUDGES 2:11–13

Secret #13
Teach your children to experience God for themselves.

Unless we teach each successive generation to experience God for themselves, Christianity is one generation from extinction. Left to the natural drift of history, Christianity is too often lost within a family by the third generation. This means that if we are not careful, our children and grandchildren may not follow God as adults.

Three Generations: Abraham, Isaac and Esau and Jacob

Abraham (initially called Abram) was a pagan shepherd living in the land of Haran. He came from a family of idolaters (Joshua 24:2, 15). Then one day the Lord appeared to him and told him to leave the land of his birth, his father's house, and his kindred and to go "to the land that I will show you" (Genesis 12:1). By faith in the Lord, Abraham left Haran with his wife, Sarah, and his nephew, Lot, and all their servants and flocks and traveled to the land of Canaan (Hebrews 11:8).

Because he had a personal encounter with God, Abraham built an altar and called upon the name of the Lord (Genesis 12:1–8). He publicly prayed and proclaimed the Lord's character and authority, and for the rest of his life, he lived the life of faith.

Abraham is a prototypical first-generation follower of God. He had a direct relationship with the Lord based on his personal experience of God's character and strength. He saw God perform a miracle by giving Sarah a baby at the age of ninety. His bold faith is evident in his decision to leave his homeland, and his total obedience is displayed by his willingness to offer his special son, Isaac, as a sacrifice (Genesis 22).

Abraham's son, Isaac, had an unremarkable spiritual journey. He is, in many ways, a typical second-generation follower of God. While Abraham's story includes the building of many altars for worship, Isaac's story centers on wells dug for water. This would seem to indicate that his life was more focused on the material than the spiritual. Like many second-generation God-followers, Isaac lacked the depth of faith and commitment of his father.

Isaac had two sons, Esau and Jacob. Esau is noted for trading his birthright for a bowl of beans—revealing that his priorities were focused on the physical and the immediate instead of the lasting and the eternal. Esau is also noted for marrying pagan wives. He became the progenitor of the Edomites. Nowhere in the Bible is he described as encountering or worshipping the Lord. Sadly, Esau is like many third-generation followers of God, in that he never met the Lord for himself.

Jacob initially also had no personal relationship with God. He is noted for stealing his brother's birthright. His relationship with the Lord was secondhand, and he referred to the Lord as the God of his father (Genesis 28:21; 32:9).

It was not until after Jacob had left home, his parents had died, and Esau was on his way with four hundred men to kill him that he got desperate enough to meet the Lord. Fortunately, this encounter with God transformed Jacob's life to such an extent that God changed Jacob's name—which means "usurper"—to Israel, meaning "God prevails" (Genesis 32:28). Jacob called the place where he met the Lord *Peniel*, which means "the face of God" (Genesis 32:30). Jacob is an example of many third-generation followers of the Lord who don't find their own relationship with God until they experience a crisis later in life.

David and His Family

David is famously referred to as a man after God's own heart (Acts 13:22). That he had an intimate personal relationship with the Lord is manifested clearly in the many psalms he wrote. He stood boldly for God and trusted the Lord to help him defeat the giant Goliath (1 Samuel 17). He experienced God's power as the Lord miraculously sent angel soldiers to fight the Philistines from the tops of the mulberry trees (2 Samuel 5:22–25).

Like many first-generation followers of God, David had a passionate personal relationship with God. He turned problems into prayers and pursued God with a hungry heart (Psalm 63). He had an exuberant love for God that came out in joyously undignified dancing when he brought the Ark of the Covenant back to Israel (2 Samuel 6:14, 22). His life was marked by radical commitment.

David had several sons, including Solomon, who succeeded him as king of Israel. After an impressive display of faith and prayer at the dedication of the temple, Solomon's spiritual life was mediocre at best. David was a wholehearted God-follower, but Solomon was halfhearted.

As Solomon grew old, his wives turned his heart after other gods, and his heart was not fully devoted to the Lord his God, as the heart of David his father had been. He followed Ashtoreth the goddess of the Sidonians, and Molek the detestable god of the Ammonites. So Solomon did evil in the eyes of the Lord; he did not follow the Lord completely, as David his father had done.

1 KINGS 11:4–6 NIV

Solomon is a classic example of a second-generation follower of God. He knew how to act godly on the outside and could pray impressive prayers in public. He was more educated and sophisticated than his shepherd-warrior father. He knew the truth (he compiled most of the book of Proverbs), but he wanted to impress the rest of the world with his wealth and power. He lived a temporally focused life, seeking satisfaction in money, sex, and power instead of in his relationship with the Lord (see the book of Ecclesiastes). He lacked the ardent personal faith of his father, and his inner life was marked by compromise and incomplete obedience.

Solomon had many sons, including Rehoboam, who succeeded him as king. Rehoboam quickly lost control of the ten tribes of Israel but remained king over Judah. There is no record of his personal relationship with the Lord. As Judah's king, he allowed the nation to worship idols (1 Kings 14:21–25). His spiritual life was marked by confusion and blatant disobedience like many third-generation followers of God.

How to Break the Tendency toward Apostasy

Take heart—second-generation mediocrity and third-generation apostasy are not an absolute certainty, just a far-too-frequent tendency. Every person has the free will to choose a life of radical devotion to the Lord God. Parents can learn from the mistakes of others and take steps to make it difficult for their children and grandchildren to abandon the Lord.

1. Parents must allow the Lord to transform every aspect of their character.

Most first-generation parents passionately love the Lord because He has rescued them from spiritual bondage. Unfortunately, the spiritual weaknesses of this generation are often magnified in the lives of their children.

For example, Abraham was called by God out of a pagan culture. On at least two separate occasions, he fudged on the truth to protect himself (Genesis 12:11–13; 20:1–2). His son Isaac continued the trait by lying to protect himself (Genesis 26:7). Ironically, Isaac's son Jacob lied to him when Jacob stole his brother's birthright.

David's sins were even more greatly magnified in his children. When he was in his mid-fifties, David gave into lust and had an adulterous affair with a married woman, Bathsheba (2 Samuel 11). To cover his sin, he had her husband killed in battle.

David's oldest son, Amnon, also gave into lust and ended up raping his beautiful half-sister Tamar. Because of David's inaction regarding the incident, another of David's sons, Absalom, murdered Amnon. Later Absalom attempted to steal his father's throne. As a sign of supposed kingly authority, he slept with David's concubines.

As parents we need to understand that our weaknesses and

sins may be magnified and multiplied in the lives of our children. We must break the tendency to pass along our weaknesses by allowing the Lord to redeem every aspect of our lives.

2. Parents must deepen their love for God and actively depend on Him.

The book of Revelation opens with seven messages from Jesus delivered to seven churches in Asia Minor (Revelation 2–3). These messages were given in the mid-90s of the modern era. The church in Ephesus was started by Paul on his third missionary journey in the mid-50s. The other churches mentioned in Revelation were started out of Ephesus. Therefore, the churches Jesus addresses in Revelation were thirty to forty years old. That means that many of the members of those churches would have been second-generation Christians.

It was the second-generation Christians in Ephesus and their parents that Jesus told to return to their "first love" (Revelation 2:4–5). They needed to rekindle a vital relationship with the Lord. To the church in Smyrna, the message was to stay faithful in spite of persecution (Revelation 2:10).

To the church in Pergamum, the message is a harsh rebuke of idolatry and immorality that was already creeping into the church (Revelation 2:14). The church in Thyatira was told to hold out against the pull toward immorality (Revelation 2:20–26).

The church in Sardis was accused of having an outward-appearing spiritual life but being dead on the inside (Revelation 3:1–3). The Philadelphian church was told to take advantage of opportunities (Revelation 3:8).

Of the seven churches, perhaps the Laodicean church is most typical of second-generation Christians. They had become spiritually lukewarm, self-sufficient, and independent of the Lord, totally unaware of the depth of their spiritual poverty (Revelation 3:15–16). Jesus told them to run zealously back to Him and open themselves up to Him (Revelation 3:19–20).

If we want to pass on to our children a spiritual vitality, we must live it and model it. Our children should see us praying, reading the Bible, praising, worshipping, serving, and evangelizing. They should not be able to escape the contagious love we have for God.

3. Parents need to take responsibility to discipline their children consistently and to stay actively connected to them.

David's ugly problems with his children were primarily the result of his refusal to discipline his children and stay actively involved in their lives. As they became adults, they were out of control. After Amnon's horrible incident of raping his half-sister, the Bible gives this sad account:

King David heard the whole story and was enraged, but he didn't
discipline Amnon. David doted on him because he was his firstborn.

2 SAMUEL 13:21 MSG

Two years later David's son Absalom invited him to come to a big party he was throwing. But despite Absalom's persistent insistence, David refused to attend. Absalom took advantage of David's parental irresponsibility and took it into his own hands to punish Amnon by having him killed.

Absalom fled for his life and lived in exile for three years until David's adviser prevailed upon him to bring Absalom back home. David did, but failed to reconcile with his son or even speak to him. Of course this built resentment in Absalom's heart. This bitterness grew until Absalom attempted an ugly military coup, which cost him his life in battle, along with the lives of thousands of soldiers.

If we hope to keep our kids connected to us and the Lord, we must stay connected with them, especially as they move into adulthood.

4. Parents must allow their children to be in situations where they can see God work for themselves.

The startling difference between the first and second generations, and the second and the third generations, as described in Joshua and Judges, was a personal experience with seeing God work. The ones who pledged their faithfulness to the Lord had seen Him work with their own eyes. Those who abandoned the Lord had not experienced His works for themselves. Our children need to experience God for themselves.

This means that we must not always keep them in "safe" Christian environments. We need to allow our children to be in situations where they will have their faith tested. They need to have opportunities to share their faith.

We must allow and encourage our children to pursue faith-challenging opportunities, such as church camps, retreats, and mission trips. Parents should serve alongside their children in Christian ministry to create common experiences of seeing the Lord work. We need to encourage our children to pray and see God answer their prayers.

We have always tried to practice lifestyle evangelism. When our children were very young, our neighbors the Lees were Buddhists. We led our boys to pray for the Lees every night and to invite the children to church with us. Cathy had the boys over to play often. They loved coming to our house.

Over time, the parents took notice of our investment. One day Mr. Lee said to me, "You can take my sons to church now and make them Christians."

My children rejoiced as they saw God answer their prayers.

At that time, our neighbors on the other side, Shaun and Kathy, also were not Christians. We led our boys to pray for them every night as well. We also tried to be good neighbors and invited them over from time to time, as well as to church. One night Cathy and I had the privilege of leading Shaun and Kathy to Christ. Our boys again got to see God answer their prayers.

A year or so later, Shaun and Kathy moved away. Our boys were ages one, three, and five years old at the time. I began praying for another non-Christian family to move in whom we could lead to Christ. Meanwhile, my boys were praying for a Christian family with children ages three and five to move in.

One day Cathy called me at work, laughing. "I just met our new neighbors," she said.

"So who won—me or the boys?" I asked.

"Well, does the name Pastor Claypool ring a bell?" she asked.

"Yes, but I am not sure how. Why?" I asked.

"He knows you," she said. "He met you at a pastor's breakfast. He's a new pastor in town to start a church. He and his wife have two children, ages three and five—and they are our new neighbors!" She laughed. "I guess God heard the prayers of a couple of little children ahead of yours!"

Our elder sons, who learned at a very young age that God answers their prayers, now lead prayer ministries at their college. They are some of the strongest prayer warriors I know. They have their own faith in God that often positively challenges me.

A Look in the Mirror

1. Are you a first-, second-, or third-generation God-follower?

2. What can you do to rekindle your own relationship with God?

3. What are you doing to help your children develop their own vibrant, personal relationships with the Lord?

4. Are you teaching your children how to study God's Word and pray expectant prayers?

5. How are you exposing your children to situations that will stretch, test, and build their faith in God?

Notes

1. http://www.hcs.harvard.edu/~gsascf/shield.html

2. I heard this concept of the three generations explained most clearly by Bruce Wilkinson in a talk he gave to the student body of Cedarville College.

14 When You Have No Other Option, Keep Praying![1]

Cathy and I have tried to do everything right as parents for our three boys. Yet they also have free wills. Each one has experienced very painful seasons of wandering from the path of wisdom. I'll spare you the details, but their wanderings have landed them in emergency rooms, hospitals, police stations, and courtrooms. But by God's great grace and magnificent mercy, each one has returned stronger as a result. But don't think it didn't nearly kill us as parents.

David Delk, president of Man in the Mirror ministries, quotes a statistic that 85 percent of children in America drop out of church before high school graduation; and of those, only 40 percent eventually return. Said another way, only 60 percent of those raised in the church will still follow Jesus as adults. That means that 40 percent of the kids you saw at church this past Sunday will grow up to become spiritual prodigals.

We all have prodigals in our lives and in our families. Even Billy and Ruth Graham, the best-known Christians of this past century, saw two of their five children live as spiritual wanderers, going through ugly seasons of rebellion, drinking, and drug abuse before eventually returning to the Lord. Another of their children experienced the pain of two broken marriages and saw her children go through a painful series of out-of-wedlock pregnancies, drug use, and eating disorders. But just as the Grahams discovered, Cathy and I have found that it is possible to pray prodigals home. Whether it is a prodigal son or daughter, mother or father, sister or brother, husband or wife, prayer is a powerful weapon for turning them around. Don't give up hope.

Lessons on Parenting from the Ultimate Father

Most people, I think, are familiar with the story of the Prodigal Son. Certainly, if you have a prodigal in your family, you are all too familiar with the details. But if you haven't read the story in a while, I encourage you to refresh your memory by reading the account in Luke 15:11–32.

The story can be read on two levels. First, it is the story of a human father and a defiant son. Second, it is the story of our heavenly Father and His rebellious children. In this parable, we can learn at least seven clear lessons from the father of the prodigal son.

1. The father gave his son the opportunity to make mistakes.
It is hard to give somebody rope when they have shown that

they might just hang themselves with it. I admire this father's willingness to let his son make mistakes.

2. The father did not let his own reputation keep him from doing what he thought was right.

If we are going to effectively minister to the prodigals in our families, we must not allow our ego or our reputation to get in the way.

3. The father refused to bail his son out of the mess he made.

This is hard. We hate to see our kids suffer. But the father wisely understood that the pain of messy circumstances is much less than the ultimate destruction brought on by an unchecked prodigal lifestyle.

4. The father did not give up hope.

As long as your prodigal is alive and kicking, there is hope.

5. The father kept the light on and the welcome mat out for the son to come home.

A college friend of mine named Drew had a dad who was the pastor of a large and influential church. In his teen years, Drew went through a rough period of rebellion. Of those years he writes:

One of the most powerful memories I have of my prodigal years in high school is of my Dad devotedly coming to my bedside at night to touch my arm, rub my forehead, and tell me he loved me. He knew my heart was far from him—and from God. And he must have known that his expressions of love would not be reciprocated, but rejected. Still he came in, sat down on my bedside, and in effect hung a "Welcome Home" sign for me.

6. *The father extended full forgiveness.*

When the son returned, the father gave unconditional forgiveness! Forgiveness does not mean that you forget the pain and hurt. It does mean that you choose not to let it affect your treatment of the offender.

7. *The father had probably been praying the whole time.*

It is not explicitly stated in the text, but it is evident. The fact that the father saw his son coming a long way off tells me that he had been praying and believing all along.

Keys to Praying for Your Prodigal Child

1. Ask God the Father to parent the prodigal.

Remember that the prodigal is one of God's own children—and He wants him or her back even more than you do. Ask God to lovingly protect and discipline the prodigal, and to draw him or her to Himself. Ask the Lord to be the Good Shepherd and rescue the prodigal as a shepherd rescues a lamb that strays from the flock.

2. Pray that you don't get bitter.

Through all the pain and insult, the father in Jesus' story refused to get bitter. Parents who have had a child rebel against them and their values can experience intense pain and despair. When they see their own children walk away from all they want for them—and especially a relationship with God—it can be as upsetting as watching them die. Ask God to give you the grace not to become bitter at God or at the prodigal.

3. Pray for the grace to let them go.

The prodigal's father did not lay a religious guilt trip on his son; he simply let him go. Pray for grace not to lay judgment on your prodigal child. Pray for grace to keep your mouth shut and your heart open with love and compassion. Pray for grace not to speak with a mouth that is critical or judgmental.

4. Pray for the endurance not to give up.

We don't know how long the prodigal son was gone. The father had a huge estate, and it may have taken years to blow through it. After the son spent all the money, he still needed to hit bottom—feeding pigs—before he returned home. It can take years to see the fruit of our intercession for a prodigal. Keep praying.

5. Pray for famine.

The prodigal son ran out of money and got hungry more quickly because there was a famine in the land. Pray that whatever, or whoever, your prodigal is placing trust in—apart from Jesus—will dry up. Pray for disillusionment toward the very things that once drew him or her into captivity. Pray that what once brought pleasure would become dry and barren. Pray that the novelty will wear off.

6. Pray for holy hunger or spiritual homesickness.

Pray that your prodigal will get *spiritually* hungry and thirsty. Pray that your prodigal will long for the relationship he or she once had with you, your family, the church, and with God the Father.

There was a time when one of my sons foolishly insisted on leaving home and doing his thing his way. Watching him leave broke our hearts. But he was nineteen years old, and there was nothing we could do. But day after day we prayed specifically that he would experience famine in relationships. We asked the Lord to protect him but let him experience emptiness. We prayed that unprofitable relationships would dry up and that he would get literally cold and hungry, such that he would want to come home.

After a couple of months, I got a phone call. The voice on the other end was humble and contrite. My son said, "Dad, can I come home?"

His "friends" had deeply disappointed him.

He had gotten *cold* when the house where he was staying had lost its heat in the teeth of winter. He had gotten *hungry* when he ran out of money, lost his job, and had nothing to eat. He came home, and within a few months he was seriously seeking God.

7. *Pray for a return of sensibility.*

Eventually the prodigal son came to his senses. The lightbulb finally went off, and the truth of his situation sunk in. Pray for your prodigal that he or she would realize that something is wrong. Pray for eyes to be opened to the truth and for protection against the delusions of the enemy.

8. Pray for gifts of repentance.

The prodigal son decided to change. He acted on his decision and went home. Repentance describes *a change of mind leading to a change of heart*, resulting in a *change of behavior.* It means "to turn and go in a new direction." Spiritual repentance is a spiritual gift. Ask the Father to give your prodigal the gift of repentance.

9. Pray that the prodigal will have the ability to receive the grace of God.

Pray that your prodigal will be able to receive the Father's love and forgiveness. Some prodigals live very immoral lives, and they can't imagine the Father ever wanting them back. They feel they have crossed some sort of line and that the Lord would not be able to bless them again.

10. Pray for "welcoming love."

The father never stopped watching and waiting, hoping and believing. Pray for a love that will be open and warm to your prodigal even when he or she is still in sin. Love does not mean condoning a prodigal's actions but does mean wanting what is best and doing what is best for him or her. It is offering acceptance and unconditional love even when you cannot condone the sinful behavior. Pray from a disposition of love, not of judgment and anger.

11. Pray that the Lord will pour out his riches when the prodigal returns.

Ask the Lord to lavish His love on the prodigal. Pray that when the prodigal returns, he or she will receive blessing upon blessing—spiritually, emotionally, physically, and financially.

Perhaps you have been praying for a prodigal son or daughter for years and nothing seems to be happening. Let me encourage you: Don't stop! Persistent prayer works. I'll tell you a prodigal story from my own family.

When my sister Carol, who is twelve years older than I am, was in high school, she was very active in the youth group at church. Then she went to college and fell in love with a young man named Don. Don was a Catholic and not yet born again. When Carol asked our pastor if she and Dan could be married in our home church, he refused. He felt that joining a Baptist and a Catholic would create an unequal yoke (1 Corinthians 6:14). This made Carol bitter, and she dropped out of church.

A few years later, the same pastor married his son, a Baptist, to a Catholic girl in our church. This made my mom bitter, and she withdrew from the fellowship of the church. She still attended the service on Sunday mornings, but she sat in the back, came late, and left early. I don't recall ever seeing her read her Bible during that time. I never heard her pray. She never spoke about spiritual things. In fact, when I told her I thought God was calling me to become a pastor, her reply was, "Oh no. Not that."

Concerned for both my mom and my sister, I put them on my daily prayer list. After years of interceding for my mom, something remarkable happened. One night when Cathy and I were meeting my parents at a restaurant for dinner, my mom walked in with a new countenance. The hard, heavy, clouded-over expression she had worn for years was replaced with a bright sunny smile. During the meal, I was shocked to hear my ultra-quiet mom speak with the waitress about her relationship with Christ. As we walked to the parking lot, my mother shocked me by putting gospel pamphlets on the windshields of the cars.

"Mom," I asked, "what on earth has happened to you?"

She told me that she had been invited to a women's small group Bible study. There she learned to let go of her bitterness and yield everything to God. She also learned to pray for my sister. When my mom came home to God, my Dad stepped up his relationship with God. Soon we were all praying regularly for Carol.

Things Get Worse

Have you ever prayed for something and things got worse before they got better? That is what happened with my sister. We had prayed for her consistently for nearly a decade when one day, out of the blue, she called a family meeting. She and Don sat on one side of the table with Mom, Dad, Cathy, and me on the other.

"From now on," Carol said, "I do not want to be considered part of this family."

We were dumbfounded to hear my sister disown us as her family. The next thing we knew, she and Don got up and left. Very shortly after that, Carol left Don and moved to another state.

We did not see Carol or hear from her for years. One day my youngest son, Luke, was looking at an old family photo album. He pointed at a picture of Carol and asked, "Daddy who is that lady with you and Mommy?"

When I told him, he said innocently, "I didn't know that you had a sister."

"I guess I don't have a sister anymore," I said.

Maybe you are more spiritual than I am, but I have to admit that I quit praying for Carol because it did not seem to be working. Fortunately, Mom and Dad did not quit. Every day, they called Carol's name out to God.

A Christmas Surprise

One Christmas Eve, as I got up to lead one of several Christmas services at our church, I looked out in the audience and was shocked by what I saw. About halfway back, on the middle aisle, sat Carol, Don, and their two daughters. We spoke with them after the service and were surprised to find that they had recently gotten back together and had moved from a town seventy-five miles away to a town fifteen minutes away.

Carol began to attend some of our family events and even began to come to our church about once a month. One Saturday while we watched my boys at a sporting event, she surprised me again.

"I think I would join your church," she said, "except for three things."

After regaining my composure, I asked, "What are the three things?"

"I think abortion is all right, I think homosexuality is okay, and I hate Jerry Falwell."

I chuckled at her third excuse, but I could see that she was serious. "Well," I said, "you have been to our church enough times to know that the big issue is Jesus Christ. What we focus on is a person's relationship with Jesus, not abortion, homosexuality, or Jerry Falwell. We believe that once you have a real relationship with the Lord, you can read the Bible and see what God thinks about abortion, homosexuality, or Jerry Falwell."

That seemed to satisfy her, and she began to come to church every Sunday morning.

"It Is Good to Be Home"

A few months later, I walked up on the platform to lead a Sunday evening celebration of the Lord's Table. When I looked out into the audience, I was shocked to see my sister sitting about halfway back on the middle aisle.

After the service, as I walked down the aisle toward the back of the sanctuary, Carol grabbed me and pulled me into a bear hug. I noticed tears on her face as she leaned in to whisper into my ear, "It's good to be home. It has been thirty years since I celebrated the Lord's Table, and it is so good to finally be home."

The Rest of the Story

A few years later, my mom went home to be with the Lord. During the last few years of her life, she had become a mighty prayer warrior. Less than five feet tall and weighing less than a hundred pounds, she prayed with a simple, direct faith that got amazing results. Now she was gone. I remember wondering who would ever take her place.

About a week later, we had a family get-together at my sister's house. Exactly as my mom had done, Carol made us all grab hands and led us in a prayer. It was eerily familiar. She prayed with simple, direct faith exactly as Mom had done.

In the years since, Carol has become quite a spiritual fireball. She has traveled the world on mission trips. She went from being in a small group Bible study to leading one, and now to coaching fifteen women's Bible study leaders.

I love to tell her story. It reminds us that it is possible to pray our prodigal loved ones home.

The Story Continues

I was speaking at a church one Friday night and concluded the message by telling how prayer had brought Mom and Carol home to God. When I gave an opportunity for people to come and pray for prodigal loved ones, many responded. One couple especially caught my attention because they seemed especially broken as they sobbed at the prayer altar.

After the service they grabbed me and told me about their nineteen-year-old daughter, Ashley, who had run away from home six weeks earlier. They did not know where she was. We prayed for God to touch Ashley's heart and call her home. I looked at my watch and prayed, "Lord, we do not know where Ashley is, but You do. Right now, at 8:33, we ask You to speak to her heart. Make her hungry for home. Bring her to her senses and call her back to You."

The parents thanked me and told me they would not be at the service the next night because of a prior commitment, but they would be back on Sunday.

The next night, as I was speaking, I noticed a young lady I had not seen there the night before. But I didn't think any more about it.

After the service, I was standing in the lobby when that same young lady ran up to me and hugged me.

Taken aback by her forwardness I asked, "Who are you?"

"I'm Ashley," she said. "Last night, at 8:33, I had an overwhelming longing to go home. I went home to Mom and Dad. Tonight I came home to God."

Note

1. This chapter was adapted from Dave Earley and Elmer Towns, *Praying for Your Children* (Shippensburg, PA: Destiny Image, 2010), 77–91.

Acknowledgments

Thanks to my friend and agent, Les Stobbe, for your great efforts in promoting my book ideas.

Thanks to Tim Martins, Paul Muckley, and others at Barbour Publishing who believed in this project and wanted to produce this book. I am grateful to many others at Barbour involved in various aspects of this project, among them Ashley Schrock for cover design and Dave Lindstedt for editing.

Thanks to many who contributed to my understanding of the Bible and parenting, including Dr. Ron Hawkins, Chuck Swindoll, and Bruce Wilkinson. Thanks to Kenneth Bailey for your contribution to my understanding of the parable of the prodigal son.

Thanks to our heavenly Father, who gives us the precious gift of children and a book that tells us what to do with them.

Our prayer, heavenly Father, is that You will use this little book to encourage, inspire, and instruct parents to raise children who will bring You great joy!

Index